Trojan Horse in the City of God

The Catholic Crisis Explained

WORKS BY DIETRICH VON HILDEBRAND

IN ENGLISH

Man and Woman†

Liturgy and Personality†

Transformation in Christ†

Jaws of Death: Gate of Heaven†

Trojan Horse in the City of God†

Marriage: The Mystery of Faithful Love†

In Defense of Purity

Fundamental Moral Attitudes

Ethics

The New Tower of Babel

Situation Ethics

Graven Images

What Is Philosophy?

Not as the World Gives

The Heart

The Devastated Vineyard

Celibacy and the Crisis of Faith

The Encyclical *Humanae Vitae*

Satan at Work

IN GERMAN

Die Idee der sittlichen Handlung

Sittlichkeit und ethische Werterkenntnis

Metaphysik der Gemeinschaft

Das katholische Berufsethos

Engelbert Dollfuss: Ein katholischer Staatsmann

Zeitliches im Lichte des Ewigen

Der Sinn philosophischen Fragens und Erkennens

Die Menschheit am Scheideweg

Mozart, Beethoven, Schubert

Heiligkeit und Tüchtigkeit

Das Wesen der Liebe

Die Dankbarkeit

Ästhetik I & II

Moralia

†*Available from Sophia Institute Press*

Dietrich von Hildebrand

Trojan Horse in the City of God

The Catholic Crisis Explained

Foreword by
John Cardinal O'Connor

SOPHIA INSTITUTE PRESS
Manchester, New Hampshire

Trojan Horse in the City of God was first published in 1967 by Franciscan Herald Press in Chicago. This 1993 edition includes a new subtitle, a new format, new chapter subtitles, and minor editorial revisions throughout. It is published by Sophia Institute Press with permission of Alice von Hildebrand.

Jacket design by Joan Barger

Sophia Institute Press
Box 5284, Manchester, NH 03108
1-800-888-9344

Nihil obstat: Marion A. Habig, O.F.M., *Censor Deputatus*
Imprimatur: Most Rev. Cletus F. O'Donnell, D.D.
Vicar General, Archdiocese of Chicago
March 8, 1967

Library of Congress Cataloging-in-Publication Data

Von Hildebrand, Dietrich, 1899-1977
Trojan horse in the city of God : the Catholic crisis explained / Dietrich von Hildebrand : foreword by John Cardinal O'Connor.
p. cm.
Includes bibliographical references.
ISBN 0-918477-18-2 : $16.95
1. Church renewal—Catholic Church. 2. Vatican Council (2nd : 1962-1965) 3. Secularization (Theology) 4. Secularism. 5. Catholic Church—History—1965- 6. Liberalism (Religion)—Catholic Church—Controversial literature. 7. Catholic Church—Doctrines. I. Title.
BX1746.V66 1993
282'.0904—dc20 93-1761 CIP

2 4 6 8 10 9 7 5 3

"It is an act of charity
to cry out against the wolf
when he is among the sheep."

St. Francis de Sales

Introduction to the Devout Life
Part III, Ch. 29

Editor's Note: The biblical quotations in the following pages are enumerated according to the Douay-Rheims edition of the Old and New Testaments. Where appropriate, quotations from the Psalms are cross-referenced with the differing enumeration in the Revised Standard Version using the following symbol: (RSV =).

Table of Contents

Part IV. Sacred and Secular

Foreword

by John Cardinal O'Connor

THE MARCH OF FOLLY, as Barbara Tuchman would define it in her book of the same name, is the "pursuit of policy contrary to self-interest."[1] Using the Trojan Horse as a prototype, she faults world governments (including such Church governance as that of the Renaissance Popes) for abdicating authority to those who would destroy society from within, be it civil or ecclesial.

The epigrammatic comments of Fr. Henri de Lubac (on page 8 of this edition of Dietrich von Hildebrand's *Trojan Horse in the City of God*), written long before the Tuchman book, express a fear that the Church has, indeed, been in danger of abdicating authority to the adversaries it has welcomed into its midst.

In no way, of course, would de Lubac ground his fear in any of the documents of the Second Vatican Council. On the contrary, he speaks of the deliberate efforts to establish a "post-Conciliar

1 Barbara W. Tuchman, *The March of Folly: from Troy to Vietnam* (New York: Alfred A. Knopf, 1984), 5.

Church," that is, a "new Church." It is not unfair to say that such efforts have exploited the Council and have disguised themselves as authentic interpretations of the Council, as the Trojan Horse was disguised as a gift from the goddess Athena but was in fact filled with Athenian soldiers bent on the destruction of Troy.

If I interpret correctly Dietrich von Hildebrand's use of the title *Trojan Horse in the City of God*, he is decrying the same distortions warned against by Henri de Lubac. Indeed, Part I of *Trojan Horse* is entitled *True and False Renewal*, and begins precisely with praise of the Fathers of the Council and the "greatness of the Second Vatican Council" itself. Yet many contemporary writings about the Council, he observes, can sadden us and fill us with grave apprehension. "On the one side," von Hildebrand writes, "we find the true spirit of Christ, the authentic voice of the Church; we find texts that in both form and content breathe a glorious supernatural atmosphere. On the other side, we find a depressing secularization, a complete loss of the *sensus supranaturalis* (sense for the supernatural), a morass of confusion" (p. 10).

My copy of von Hildebrand's *Trojan Horse* is the revised edition of 1967. The official documents of the Council, sixteen of them, were published in 1965. It would not be unfair to ask whether von Hildebrand's critique of distorted interpretations and the invasion of the Church by secularism, which might have been accurate in describing the early years of turbulence following the Council, is apt for 1993. I believe it is equally apt for 1993, unfortunately because so many of his warnings were ignored and ridiculed in 1967.

It is my own repeated reminder to all who will listen that but a minority of Catholics have a familiarity with the actual documents of the Second Vatican Council. I fear that the same lack of familiarity characterizes many who speak glibly of the *spirit* of the Council, dismissing with near-contempt those who suggest what the Fathers of the Council actually *said*. This, twenty-eight years after the publication of the documents!

Quite apart from the perduring ignorance of the documents of the Second Vatican Council (which alone should make a new publication of von Hildebrand's book welcome) is the perduring power of secularism. It is against secularism that von Hildebrand inveighs most strongly and consistently. It is the invasion of secularism into the life of the Church that he sees as most analogous to the invasion of Troy by the Athenians. "To be sure," he says, "secularization is an evil primarily because it implies an apostasy from Christ, and it is for this reason that we fight it on every page of this book." He adds what anyone struggling in the ecumenical movement today, as am I, must recognize as a profound insight: "secularization stands in the way of true and authentic ecumenism" (p. 220).

I hope that the republication of *Trojan Horse in the City of God* will win many new readers. And I hope further that they will take special note of Dietrich von Hildebrand's quoting John Henry Cardinal Newman about the Church: "She holds that unless She can, in Her own way, do good to souls, it is no use Her doing anything" (p. 266). That quotation is found in the Epilogue to *Trojan Horse*. It synthesizes von Hildebrand's primary message throughout this work, a message critically needed today.

Acknowledgment

I wish to express my great and deep indebtedness to my dear friend William Fitzpatrick of Rutgers University who, with the greatest devotion and loving intelligence, has helped me edit this manuscript.

I also want to thank my beloved wife, my constant collaborator, without whose help this book would never have been written.

Dietrich von Hildebrand
New Rochelle, 1967

Trojan Horse in the City of God

The Catholic Crisis Explained

Author's Introduction

IF WE CONSIDER certain things that Kierkegaard has to say about faith, about the fundamental religious attitude, and if we then turn to a number of articles by Catholic priests and laymen published in recent years, we cannot escape the impression that these writers not only have lost their Catholic faith, but also no longer understand the very nature of religion based on divine revelation.

Indeed, we are tempted to ask if these so-called "progressive Catholics" ever had a true religious experience, if they ever experienced the elementary confrontation with the absolute Lord: the fear and trembling before the infinitely holy God and the blissful encounter with Christ, the Epiphany of God. Are they capable of understanding the words of Pascal's *Memorial:*

God of Abraham, God of Isaac, God of Jacob,
not the God of philosophers and learned men.
Certitude. Certitude. Feeling, joy, peace.
God of Jesus Christ.
My God and your God.

Your God will be my God.
Forgetfulness of the world and of all save God.
He is not only to be found through the ways taught in the Gospel.
Greatness of the human soul.
Just Father, the world has not known You, but I have known You.
Joy, joy, joy, tears of joy.
I have separated myself from Him.
They have abandoned me, the source of living water.
My God, wilt Thou leave me?
Let me not be separated from Him eternally.

This is eternal life, knowing Thee the only true
God and Him who Thou hast sent, Jesus Christ.
Jesus Christ.
Jesus Christ.
I have separated myself from Him.
I have run away from Him, denied Him, crucified Him.
May I never be separated from Him!
He is only to be kept through the ways taught in the Gospel.
Renunciation, total and sweet.
Total surrender to Jesus Christ and my spiritual director.
Eternally joyful for one single day of renunciation on Earth.
I shall not forget your words.
Amen.[2]

This book is addressed to all those who are still aware of the metaphysical situation of man, to those who have resisted brainwashing by secular slogans, who still possess the longing for God and are still conscious of a need for redemption. It is addressed to

[2] Translated from the French in *Oeuvres complètes*, ed. Jacques Chevalier, Bibliothèque de la Pléiade (Paris: Éditions Gallimard, 1954), 554.

those who have not yet become deaf to the voice of Christ amid the noisy huckstering of cheap and shallow formulas, to those whose minds are not spellbound by the alleged *coming of age of modern man*, to those not caught in the turmoil of the contemporary "puberty crisis." This book seeks to appeal to those in whom a sense of real depth and grandeur is to be found, to those who can still see the abyss that separates a Plato from a Russell, a Shakespeare from a Brecht, a Newman from a Robinson.

We are convinced that the great majority of Catholics have not yet been confused by slogans, that they are not yet swimming in the typical pride that rests on the immature illusion that man has come of age. We are furthermore convinced that many outside the Church hold to the true realism concerning man's metaphysical situation — realism that can also be found in Plato's *Phaedo* and *Phaedrus*. We mean the consciousness of the mysterious rupture in man's nature, of his being simultaneously "but a reed, the most feeble thing in nature"[3] and the lord of creation. This is a realism that does not overlook the inner conflict in man, but senses that man is in need of redemption.

Against this background we shall try to shed some light on the confusions, the apostasies, and the disclosures of loss of faith that are to be found among those who trumpet forth the claim that they are the true interpreters of the Council. Against the background of true realism, of the very core of religion, of the good tidings of the Gospel, we shall try to examine all the horrible errors that are being propagated now by the so-called progressives.

May God grant us grace so that our minds may again be enlightened by Christ, the divine truth, and our hearts be inebriated by the ineffable holiness of the God-man. May God grant

[3] Blaise Pascal, *Pensées*, trans. W.F. Trotter, vol. 33 of *The Great Books of the Western World* (Chicago: Encyclopaedia Britannica, 1952), VI, 347.

Catholics the grace to experience again what is written in the Preface of the Christmas Mass: "By the mystery of the Word made flesh, from Thy brightness a new light hath risen to shine on the eyes of our soul in order that, God becoming visible to us, we may be borne upward to the love of things invisible."

If this book contributes in a modest way to dispelling the choking fog of secularization and to opening the eyes of souls to the glory of Christ and true unity with the Church, I should consider it the greatest unmerited gift of God:

> *Despise not thy people, O almighty God,*
> *When they cry out in their affliction, but graciously*
> *Succor them in their tribulation for the glory of*
> *Thy name, through our Lord Jesus Christ.*

Part I

True and False Renewal

It is clear that the Church is facing a grave crisis. Under the name of "the new Church," "the post-Conciliar Church," a different Church from that of Jesus Christ is now trying to establish itself: an anthropocentric society threatened with immanentist apostasy which is allowing itself to be swept along in a movement of general abdication under the pretext of renewal, ecumenism, or adaptation.

Henri de Lubac, S.J.

in *Témoinage Chrétien*
(Paris, September 1, 1967)

1

False alternatives

WHEN ONE READS the luminous encyclical *Ecclesiam Suam* of Pope Paul VI or the magnificent "Dogmatic Constitution on the Church"[4] of the Fathers of the Council, one cannot but realize the greatness of the Second Vatican Council.

False interpretations of the Second Vatican Council

But when one turns to so many contemporary writings — some by very famous theologians, some by minor ones, some by laymen offering us their dilettante theological concoctions — one can only be deeply saddened and even filled with grave apprehension. For it would be difficult to conceive a greater contrast than that between the official documents of Vatican II and the superficial, insipid pronouncements of various theologians and laymen that have broken out everywhere like an infectious disease.

4 *Lumen Gentium*.

On the one side, we find the true spirit of Christ, the authentic voice of the Church; we find texts that in both form and content breathe a glorious supernatural atmosphere. On the other side, we find a depressing secularization, a complete loss of the *sensus supranaturalis*, a morass of confusion.

The distortion of the authentic nature of the Council produced by this epidemic of theological dilettantism expresses itself chiefly in the false alternatives between which we are all commanded to choose: either to accept the secularization of Christianity or to deny the authority of the Council.

The true meanings of *conservative* and *progressive*

These drastic alternatives are frequently labeled the *progressive* and *conservative* responses. These terms, facilely applied to many natural realms, can be extremely misleading when applied to the Church. It is of the very nature of Catholic Christian faith to adhere to an unchanging divine revelation, to acknowledge that there is something in the Church that is above the ups and downs of cultures and the rhythm of history. Divine revelation and the Mystical Body of Christ differ completely from all natural entities. To be conservative, to be a traditionalist, is in this case an essential element of the response due to the unique phenomenon of the Church. Even a man in no way conservative in temperament and in many other respects progressive must be conservative in his relation to the infallible magisterium of the Church, if he is to remain an orthodox Catholic. One can be progressive and simultaneously a Catholic, but one cannot be a progressive in one's Catholic faith. The idea of a "progressive Catholic" in this sense is an oxymoron, a *contradictio in adjecto*. Unfortunately, there are many today who no longer understand this contradiction and proudly proclaim themselves to be "progressive Catholics."

Conservative and progressive are false alternatives

With the labels *conservative* and *progressive* they are in fact requiring the faithful to choose between opposition to any renewal, opposition even to the elimination of things that have crept into the Church because of human frailty (e.g., legalism, abstractionism, external pressure in questions of conscience, grave abuses of authority in monasteries) and a change, a "progress" in the Catholic faith which can only mean its abandonment.

These are false alternatives. For there is a third choice, which welcomes the official decisions of the Vatican Council but at the same time emphatically rejects the secularizing interpretations given them by many so-called progressive theologians and laymen.

True renewal calls us to transformation in Christ

This third choice is based on unshakable faith in Christ and in the infallible magisterium of His Holy Church. It takes it for granted that there is no room for change in the divinely revealed doctrine of the Church. It admits no possibility of change except that development of which Cardinal Newman speaks: the explicit formulation of what was implicit in the faith of the Apostles or of what necessarily follows from it.

This attitude holds that the Christian morality of holiness, the morality revealed in the Sacred Humanity of Christ and His commandments and exemplified in all the saints, remains forever the same. It holds that being transformed in Christ, becoming a new creature in Him, is the goal of our existence. In the words of St. Paul, "This is the will of God, your sanctification."[5]

[5] 1 Thess. 4:3.

This position maintains that there is a radical difference between the kingdom of Christ and the *saeculum* (world); it takes into account the struggle between the spirit of Christ and the spirit of Satan through all the centuries past and to come, until the end of the world. It believes that Christ's words are as valid today as in any former time: "Had you been of the world, the world would love its own; but as you are not of the world, as I have chosen you out of the world, the world hates you."[6]

This is simply the Catholic position, without further qualification. It rejoices in any renewal that enlarges the establishment of all things in Christ — the *instaurare omnia in Christo* — and that brings the light of Christ to added domains of life. This is in fact a specific encouragement to Catholics to confront all things with the Spirit and Truth of Christ — in season and out of season — regardless of the spirit of the present age or any past age. Such a renewal follows the admonition of St. Paul: "Test all things; hold to what is good."[7] It appreciates reverently those great gifts of previous Christian centuries which reflect the sacred atmosphere of the Church (for example, Gregorian Chant and the admirable hymns of the Latin Liturgy).

The Catholic position maintains that these gifts should never cease to play a great role in our Liturgy and that they have today as in the past a great apostolic mission. It believes that the *Confessions* of St. Augustine, the writings of St. Francis of Assisi, and the mystical works of St. Teresa of Avila contain a vital message for *all* periods in history. It represents an attitude of deep filial devotion to the Holy Father and reverent love for the Church in all its aspects, the true *sentire cum ecclesia*.

[6] John 15:19.

[7] 1 Thess. 5:21.

It should be clear that this third response to the contemporary crisis in the Church is not timidly compromising, but consistent and forthright. It is not retrospective, nor does it anticipate a mere earthly future, but it is focused on eternity. It is thus able to live fully in the present, because real presence is fully experienced only when we succeed in freeing ourselves from the tension of past and future, only when we are no longer imprisoned in a frantic propulsion toward the next moment. In the light of eternity every moment in life — whether of an individual or a community — receives its full significance. We can do justice to the present age, therefore, only by regarding it in the light of man's eternal destiny — in the light of Christ.

The response that we have been describing involves grave concern and apprehension over the present invasion of the life of the Church by secularism. It considers the present crisis the most serious one in the entire history of the Church. Yet it is full of hope that the Church will triumph, because our Lord Himself has said: "The gates of Hell shall not prevail against it."[8]

[8] Matt. 16:18.

2

The meaning of the Council

THE MAIN THEME and end of the Council is set forth in the "Constitution on the Church." The Council "desires now to unfold more fully to the faithful of the Church and to the whole world its own inner nature and universal mission. This it intends to do following faithfully the teaching of previous Councils."[9]

The Church needs periodic renewal

It is of the nature of the Church that there be not only a growth in the dogmatic formulation of revealed truth, but also periodic reform, a renewal of Her authentic life which is always one and identical. Throughout the two thousand years of Her life, the Councils of the Church have testified to this supernatural rhythm. It involves, on the one hand, the refutation of heresies, which are continually trying to invade the Church, and, correlatively, an

[9] *Lumen Gentium*, Dogmatic Constitution on the Church, Ch. 1, "The Mystery of the Church," section 1.

increasingly explicit dogmatic formulation of revealed truth, a process described by Cardinal Newman in his *Essay on the Development of Christian Doctrine*.

On the other hand, this supernatural rhythm involves a renewal which is comparable to the various reforms that have occurred in the religious orders, such as the reform of Cluny in the Benedictine order or the reform of St. Bernardine in the Franciscan order.

Neither growth nor reform implies any alteration or evolution of the essence of the Church in the course of history. On the contrary, this supernatural rhythm of growth and renewal is the very opposite of the movement of the Hegelian world spirit in history. It is something utterly different from an adaptation of the Church to the spirit of an era. It is to be found only in the life of the Church; it springs from Her supernatural vitality.

Renewal restores the supernatural vitality of the Church

The process of renewal is a shedding of secularizing influences which, because of human frailty and the trends and tendencies of an era, have slipped into the practice of the Church and the religious life of the faithful.

As such, it is the very opposite of an evolution or progression. Rather, it is a returning to the essential and authentic spirit of the Church, a process of purification and restoration. It is a dramatic manifestation of the war between the spirit of the world (in the meaning of the Gospels) and the Spirit of Christ — which St. Augustine described as the *battle of the two cities*. In this process all views and practices that are incompatible with Christ are continually eliminated. Such was the reform of St. Gregory VII; such were the reforms of numerous Councils, especially the Council of Trent.

The Second Vatican Council sought to overcome legalism

But whereas the renewal of former Councils stressed the fight against secularizing influences that took the form of general laxity, Vatican II sought a liberation from secularization in the form of narrowness, a rejuvenation intended to overcome a certain ossification and legalism that have tended to obscure the authentic face of the Church.

This is a new dimension of renewal. However, we must emphasize that it implies neither a diminishing nor the slightest blurring of the radical antagonism that exists between the Church and the *saeculum*, the Spirit of Christ and the spirit of the world.[10]

The overcoming of narrowness is not a compromise with the times; rather it is an achievement of that breadth and freedom which only the Spirit of Christ can give, a breadth which includes the reconciliation of opposites — the *coincidentia oppositorum* — proper to the supernatural. An example of this exclusively supernatural reconciliation is the Church's rigorous exclusion of all errors (and the anathema pronounced on all that is incompatible with Christ) coupled with its loving, motherly attitude toward the

[10] "He who would interpret the Council as loosening the former engagements of the Church toward Her faith, Her tradition, Her asceticism, Her charity, Her spirit of sacrifice, and Her adherence to the Word and to the Cross of Christ, or even as an indulgent concession to the fragile and versatile relativistic mentality of a world without principles or a transcendent end, a kind of more facile and less exacting Christianity, would be completely mistaken." His Holiness Pope Paul VI (as quoted in Michel de Saint Pierre, *Sainte Colère* [Paris: Editions de la Table Ronde, 1965]: "*Quiconque verrait dans le Concile un relâchement des engagements antérieurs de l'Eglise, envers sa foi, sa tradition, son ascèse, sa charité, son espirit de sacrifice et son adhésion à la Parole et à la Croix du Christ, ou encore une indulgente concession à la fragile et versatile mentalité relativiste d'un monde sans principes et sans fin transcendante, à une sorte de christianisme plus commode et moins exigeant, ferait erreur.*")

one who errs, its respect for his personal dignity, and its eagerness to do justice to every grain of truth contained in his error. Or again, there is the clear-cut distinction between sacred and profane coupled with the penetration of everything by the Spirit of Christ, the *instaurare omnia in Christo*.

3

Thesis - antithesis

WHEN EXPRESSING our deep concern over the grave errors widespread among progressive Catholics, we sometimes meet with the response, "Well, this had to come. It is a strong reaction against former errors, abuses, and shortcomings. After a certain time, this reaction will lose its virulence and the right position will be reached."

Such an attitude seems to us very unsatisfactory because it is based on a false conception of the process by which man enlarges his conquest of basic metaphysical and moral truths. And, more serious yet, the consolation this response offers betrays a complete misunderstanding of the unique development in the detailed formulation of divine revelation by the infallible Church.

We shall deal with the former error first.

Truth is not a mean between extremes

The erroneous notion that truth is acquired when the pendulum goes from one extreme to another and finally comes to rest in the middle is based on a popular interpretation of the Hegelian dialectic of thesis, antithesis, and synthesis. But even in its esoteric form (and whatever may be its application to the rhythm of history), this dialectic certainly does not describe the process by which truth is attained. The final synthesis need by no means be any closer to truth than the thesis or antithesis.

Obviously, we are not here concerned with the case of a clearly erroneous thesis, the contradictory antithesis of which is necessarily true. For example, the claim that objective truth does not exist is an outright error. Its contradictory antithesis — namely, "There is objective truth" — is true. In this case, a synthesis of thesis and antithesis is out of the question since the two propositions are contradictories. But our subject concerns *contraries*: propositions that can *both* be erroneous.

The popular understanding of the Hegelian dialectic is that it is inevitable for the human mind to go to one extreme, then to react toward the opposite extreme, and finally to reach truth which lies midway between the two extremes.

We must distinguish two propositions that are implied in this idea: first, that history comprises a dialectical movement in which one epoch reacts diametrically against the preceding one with a resultant movement to the center position; second, that this endpoint of the movement of the pendulum, this mean between two extremes, constitutes the truth or at least a progress in the discovery of truth. It is with this second proposition that we are primarily concerned.

It assumes, for instance, that when in one epoch authority is overstressed, it will be followed by a strong reaction which emphasizes freedom and tries to do away with authority. After these two extremes of the pendulum, the resultant position will be in the center and justice will therefore be done to both authority and freedom.

Now, the idea of the mean as the *happy medium* applies to many instances of rational choice. For example, food should be neither too salty nor saltless; the temperature in a room should be neither too hot nor too cold. When, however, it comes to the exploration of truth, to philosophical controversies, to antithetical approaches to the world, or to opposed world views, the theory of the happy mean does not apply.

Extremes are not incomplete truths

In these questions the truth lies *above* the two extremes, not *between* them. In every extreme there is a wandering from the truth into error. Although the reciprocal extremes seem to be completely antagonistic, they actually share the same crucial error. The true position differs from both extremes much more than they differ from each other.

For example, in the period of liberal individualism the reality and value of community was to a great extent overlooked. This conception of man was later replaced by an overemphasis on community which reduced the role of the individual to a mere part of a whole and made his value dependent on his contribution to the community. In contrast to the nineteenth century, the mentality of the first half of the twentieth century emphasized community to the detriment of the individual person. The ideals and ideas of collectivism made great progress, especially after World War I, quite apart from the fact that Communism, Fascism, and National Socialism were sustained by brutal force in various parts of Europe.

Now, the point for our purposes is that individualism and collectivism are not two extremes between which lies the truth. In reality, the individual person and the community are so linked that it is impossible to do justice to the real nature of the person or the community whenever one is emphasized at the expense of the other. If we lose sight of their deep interrelationship we necessarily blind ourselves even to the nature and rank of the one that is overstressed. *Extremes are not incomplete truths*. Contrary to widespread belief, individualism does not overrate the value and dignity of the individual person, nor does collectivism overrate the community. On the contrary, both actually lose sight of the true essence, value, and dignity of the person *and* the community.

Far from being a doctrine that at least does justice to the value of the individual man, individualism is rather the result of a denial of the essential features of the human person. In a process that began in the Renaissance, the conception of the person was progressively stripped of its essential features. Numerous truths were denied: first, man's being ordered to God and his destiny of eternal union with Him; then, the immortality of the soul; then, the capacity for an authentic knowledge of reality; then, the substantiality of the soul; then, free will, and so on. The process began with the ambition of making man into a God and ended by making him a more highly developed animal or even a bundle of sensations. It is not surprising that in the course of this drift, man's essential capacity to enter into deep communion with others and to build a community with them was forgotten.

A similar destructive result followed from the reaction to individualism in the idolization of the community. All understanding of the nature of true community was lost and a mere collective (conceived after the pattern of material substances) was substituted for it.

Since individualism and collectivism are not, therefore, merely one-sided emphases on the individual or the community but rather distortions of the very entities they erect into idols, the truth can never be a mean between them, to be reached when the pendulum comes to rest in the middle or when a moderate individualism is combined with a moderate collectivism. The error which is at the basis of both ideologies can be overcome only by rising above the level on which these positions are antagonistic and discovering a truth above them that cannot be regarded as a synthesis of prior thesis and antithesis.

This truth will differ much more from both than they do from each other. If we consider the elaboration of the unique value of the individual person in Augustine's *Confessions* and the exposition of the glory of communion and community in his *City of God*, we see that the true view of the individual person and the community is in no way a mean between individualism and collectivism.

This example, to which numerous others could be added, may suffice to show that the above-mentioned theses and antitheses are not incomplete truths, but caricatures and misunderstandings of the nature and value of the entities they would exalt.

Overreaction to error does not yield truth

It is therefore a serious mistake to belittle the grave errors which have crept in among many Catholics by interpreting them as *natural reactions* to former errors and to console oneself with the anticipation that a resolution of action and reaction will eventually reach the truth in the center.

The illusion of the progressive Catholics is yet more simplistic. They believe that the reaction against former errors or shortcomings is itself the attainment of truth.

It is a most absurd form of naiveté to proclaim the currently reigning antithesis to errors of a former epoch as a victory of truth and a sign of remarkable progress. Of men with illusions about their own reactions to former epochs one could say — to vary a remark Talleyrand is said to have made of the Bourbons — that they have forgotten everything and learned nothing. By looking back at previous centuries they could easily discover that the various antitheses were in no way better than the preceding theses. But this is not done. They usually submit to the illusion that the present antithetical reaction to something in the preceding epoch is a breakthrough to truth.

Truth is above the rhythm of history

Our progressives tend to absolutize the views of the present age. We shall discuss below the task of the true philosopher in any age, and especially in our age — namely, to free himself from the rhythm of more or less automatic reaction and ascend to the truth which is above all antagonisms between present and former epochs. Unfortunately, some philosophers today see the mission of philosophy to be the conceptual formulation of the trends and tendencies that are "in the air" in their own age. Thus, they play the present off against the past (and can enjoy thereby feelings of contempt for previous ages), instead of pursuing their true vocation as philosophers by seeking truth above the rhythm of history.

The Church's essential nature never changes

But it suggests far greater spiritual and intellectual confusion to attempt to submit to this alternating rhythm the Church in Her supernatural nature as the Mystical Body of Christ, in Her infallible magisterium, and in the stream of grace granted to humanity through the sacraments.

The unfolding of the plenitude of divine revelation over the centuries in a movement from the implicit to the explicit is just the opposite of a rhythm of thesis and antithesis which swings from one extreme to another. It is rather an organic growth under the guidance of the Holy Spirit, in which, in the process of preserving one and the same divine revelation from all error and heresy, the glorious deposit of Catholic faith is given a more and more explicit formulation.

Notwithstanding their differences in personality and historical circumstances, the saints of all centuries manifest the same quality of holiness, the same transformation in Christ. In the diverse personalities of such saints as St. Peter, St. Augustine, St. Francis of Assisi, St. Catherine of Siena, St. Vincent de Paul, the Curé of Ars, or Don Bosco, we find the same flavor of holiness, the same glorious reflection of the Sacred Humanity of Christ, the same sublimity of a supernatural morality that surpasses any mere natural morality, even that most noble one of Socrates.

The Church's human dimension is affected by history

But the Church also has a human, natural aspect. Insofar as it is a human institution composed of frail men, it, too, is exposed to the influence of this alternating rhythm of history. Therefore the Church has the continual mission of rejecting all such influences and presenting anew to humanity the untarnished plenitude of divine truth and authentic Christian life — that is, the real message of Christ to all men.

4

False reactions

BY AND LARGE, progressive Catholics represent a mere reaction to the narrowness and legalism of a former age. This reaction is all the more false and evil because the kind of change called for in the Church today is mainly the completion of an incomplete truth or the replacement of an ambiguous formulation by an unequivocal one. We have seen that truth is *above* a wrong thesis and antithesis, and not a mere synthesis of them; and that it is *above* a wrong action and an *equally* (or more) *wrong* reaction, and not the mean between them. Therefore it is all the more naive to believe that the truth consists in a reaction to past errors.

An incomplete truth is not an error

But all this has even greater application when, instead of a *wrong thesis*, an *incomplete truth* is at issue. It is most important to see that an incomplete truth is not an error. With regard to the question of man's freedom, for example, determinism is simply a dramatic error. It is not an incomplete truth. On the other hand, the assertion that man is endowed with free will is a great truth. But it is incomplete as long as it is not also seen that this freedom must be distinguished from arbitrariness and as long as the distinction between ontological and moral freedom is not understood.

Of course, the degree of incompleteness may vary a good deal. In certain cases, incompleteness is the normal concomitant of the discovery of any truth, for many other equally important aspects of the same being or topic remain to be seen. This incompleteness can also appear as incorrectness when the incomplete truth is not adequate to the particular question it claims to answer. Indeed, it gives birth to errors whenever it claims to be complete.

But here, progress in the conquest of truth consists in completing the incomplete truth, and not in replacing it with its opposite. An opposite reaction is much worse than the former incomplete truth, for not only will it stress something equally incomplete, but in explicitly denying the former incomplete truth it will introduce an express error. Plato's insight that the soul is distinct from and ontologically superior to the body is a fundamental truth. It is incomplete in that full justice is not done to the role and value of the body. But Plato's insight remains fundamentally true despite its incompleteness; and if one reacts against this incompleteness by reducing the soul to a mere epiphenomenon of bodily processes, one actually enunciates a blatant error.

Even where the incompleteness is more serious and perhaps even dangerous, asserting merely the opposite position may represent anything but real progress. For example, in placing emphasis on the nature of the soul (the *res cogitans* or thinking thing) and its distinctness from matter (the *res extensa* or extended thing), Descartes overlooked the phenomenon of life and saw animals as mere automatons. But Bergson, in attempting to do full justice to the phenomenon of life, failed to distinguish adequately the spiritual person. This was certainly no improvement. The same must be said about the reaction to Descartes' concept of the soul as a *res cogitans* — an inadequacy that has rightly been called *chosisme*.[11] To react against the inadequacy of *chosisme* by denying the substantiality of the soul is to fall into a profound error.

To repeat: an incomplete truth is not an error, and the reaction of merely championing the opposite thesis leads not to a complete truth but to error. In the light of this analysis, we shall now examine the false reactions propagated by Catholic thinkers in the name of overcoming the narrowness of former epochs.

The incomplete truth about marriage

The traditional conception of marriage contains an incomplete truth. The exaggerated, well-nigh exclusive emphasis on procreation led to a grave and almost total neglect of the role of mutual love. Through the centuries, theologians (with the exception of St. Francis de Sales) omitted any mention of the specific nature of spousal love and its profound importance for marriage. It was a great merit of Pope Pius XII that he found the most fitting words for the nature and value of this special kind of love.

Although stress on procreation as a great and noble end was right, one can do justice to the nature of marriage only if one also grasps its significance and high value as a love communion, as the ultimate union of two persons. Further, the mystery of procreation itself can be adequately seen only against the background of the communion of love, issuing superabundantly from this love union.

It is clear, therefore, that the doctrine stressing procreation exclusively is an incomplete truth. It needs completion with a doctrine that also calls attention to the value of human love.

11 "Thing-ism," from the French for *thing*, "*chose*."

But in their books and articles, progressive Catholics all too frequently do not present the completion which found its expression in the most eloquent addresses of Pius XII, but rather a mere diametrical reaction to the former exclusive stress on procreation. And not only is the moral difference between artificial contraception and natural family planning no longer seen, but spousal love in its deepest sense is denied its rightful place, despite all the frenetic raving about it. The mystery of sex is missed because it is reduced to a merely biological instinct explained in terms of hygiene or a superficial psychology of self-fulfillment. As we have insisted in several books, however, sex can be properly understood only as sub-ordered to love, as an expression and fulfillment of spousal love.[12] The false interpretation of sex opens the door to numerous unfortunate errors concerning marriage, including even the denial of its indissolubility.

Salvation of self and salvation of neighbor are not opposed

In the past, another incompleteness with its own attendant confusion was found in such formulations as, "God and my soul alone matter; all other things are only means." This attitude was found in ascetic books and gained currency in the lives of many pious Catholics, especially among members of religious orders.

The advice to think only of God and our own sanctification and to consider everything else as a means certainly did not exclude the love of neighbor, because this love is essential to our

[12] The vanishing sense of the terrible sin of impurity among progressive Catholics clearly demonstrates that neither the real nature of spousal love nor the character of the marital act as a mutual, personal self-donation is understood. See my book *Purity* (Steubenville: Franciscan University Press, 1989). For Pius XII on marriage, see Michael Chinigo, ed., *The Pope Speaks: the Teachings of Pope Pius XII*, (N.Y.: Pantheon, 1957), 20-45.

sanctification. Without it our own sanctification would be impossible. But while it is true that the glorification of God must be the ultimate concern of each one of us, still, other persons can never be looked upon as mere means. We should also burn for our neighbor's salvation and sanctification *propter seipsum*, for his own sake, out of love for him. This is clearly expressed in Christ's commandment to love God above all things "*and thy neighbor as thyself*."[13] Our love for our neighbor is thus not even exclusively for the glorification of God, although this obviously should have absolute primacy.

Now a typical wrong reaction to the former incomplete truth is the theory Gregory Baum advanced in *Commonweal*. Whereas in former times, he says, God and the soul were alone given attention, now one's *exclusive* concern should be the salvation of one's neighbor. This point is by no means the needed completion of the incomplete truth, but rather, a mere reaction. It amounts to an opposite and equally grave (indeed, graver) error.

God is always the main theme: my sanctification and my neighbor's are equally important because both glorify God. In this sublime sphere, the categories of altruism and egotism do not apply. Because the glorification of God should have precedence over everything else, and because my own sanctification glorifies God as much as my neighbor's, it is entitled to equal consideration.

It remains true, moreover, that every man's primary task is his own (rather than his neighbor's) salvation. My chief task is to avoid offending God by sin and to glorify God through my own sanctification. This is evident from the simple fact that my control over my own transformation in Christ is immeasurably greater than my influence over that of anyone else. It is in my power, with

[13] Mark 12:31; Luke 10:27; Rom. 13:9.

the help of grace, to keep myself from offending God, but it is not in my power to keep my neighbor from doing so.

The right relation between love of God and neighbor

Another misinterpretation of the meaning of charity for one's neighbor often put forward by pious, well-intentioned Catholics assumed that it was more perfect, more supernatural, more Christian, and more pleasing to God if all the good one did to one's neighbor and all the sacrifices made in order to help him were done with the exclusive intention of following Christ's commands *and* with a complete indifference toward the other person as such.

This attitude was seen as flowing exclusively out of love of Christ, and no interest in the individual person of the neighbor was supposed to accompany our love of Christ and thereby detract from our complete self-donation to Him. One could hear such assurances as, "Believe me, I do it exclusively for Christ. This sick man as such in no way concerns me."

Obviously, there is a great and decisive difference between love of neighbor and all other natural kinds of love (such as parental love, filial love, spousal love, and friendship). Our neighbor is potentially every human being whether he attracts us or not, whether we like him or not, and whatever his character may be. In a given situation he finds himself in need or danger, or he asks something of us; he becomes our neighbor.

But the difference between love of neighbor and any other human love, great as it may be in many respects, in no way precludes an express interest in his welfare, a real *intentio benevolentiae* (good will) toward this unique individual person. On the contrary, this is precisely what makes it possible to call our love of neighbor *love:* the unique warmth for him, the bestowing of a breath of goodness on him, the sheltering embrace of his soul, the triumphant clinging to what is objectively good for him, regardless of whether he responds with good or evil.

Only Christ enables us to love our neighbor

Of course, it is a fundamental truth that this real love of neighbor, which is *charity* in the Pauline sense, is possible only as the fruit of our love of God in Christ and through Christ. Between charity and a mere humanitarian love of neighbor there yawns an abyss. Here it may suffice to stress that the irresistible, victorious goodness of charity, which is incarnate in Christ, can live only in one whose heart has been melted by Christ, whose soul has received the imprint of Christ. Only he can have genuine charity who loves God with all his soul and mind and who sees every human being in the light of Christ's revelation. I am not referring here to the exclusively supernatural aspect of charity, which we know by faith to be infused in our soul in Baptism, but rather to the very quality of the act of charity which, for everyone who has a sense of the supernatural, is visible in Christ's Sacred Humanity and in all the saints and which distinguishes charity from any humanitarian love. This quality can be realized in a man's soul only as a response of love to God in and through Christ.

Let it be understood that there would be no reason for this loving response to an evil man — one repulsive, mean, and brutal — if we did not see him in the light of Christ's revelation as a being created by God with an immortal soul for whom Christ died on the Cross. There is no other possible motivation for this love.

To love Christ, we must love our neighbor

This discussion of the nature of charity should expose the grave shortcoming in approaching one's neighbor only as an occasion for performing an act of obedience required by Christ. The very glory of charity, of which St. Paul speaks so admirably, implies a real, full interest in one's neighbor. The drastically incomplete interpretation of love for the sake of Christ has made love of neighbor a mere *behaving as if* we loved him. Christ, however, did not say, "Behave as if you love him" but "Love your neighbor as yourself." To treat one's neighbor as no more than an occasion for actualizing our obedience to Christ and performing a meritorious deed is thus in reality no true charity; it is not even obedient to Christ's commandment, because it does not realize its full content. It is necessary, therefore, when interpreting Christ's words, "What you have done to the least of my brethren, you have done to me,"[14] to remember that the individual person, our neighbor, is endowed with preciousness because Christ loves him with an infinite love and died for him on the Cross.

Love of neighbor is not love of Christ

But unfortunately, here again the progressive Catholics would replace an imperfect attitude of the past with a much more dangerous one. In order to emphasize the genuine interest we should take in our neighbor as an individual person, they interpret "What you have done to the least of my brethren you have done to me" to mean that the *only* way we can find Christ is in our neighbor.[15] The love that is a response to Christ Himself, to the infinitely holy one, the epiphany of God, is replaced by the love of neighbor. The result is that love of God is relegated to the background — if it

[14] Matt. 25:40.

[15] It is quite commonplace today to hear in sermons that our love of God can manifest itself only in our love of neighbor. See the article by William Fitzpatrick, *Triumph*, 1, No. 4 (December 1966).

does not completely disappear. This interpretation obviously introduces a most extreme error, because it ignores the first commandment, to love God, and this, after all, holds the first place. Wrong as it is to restrict love exclusively to God and to deny real love to one's neighbor, it is still much worse to exclude direct love of God.

Moreover, Christ's pronouncement that we find Him in every neighbor loses all its meaning if we do not understand that by these words Christ makes it possible for us to love our neighbor, even if we have no reason to love him for his character. That every man is precious, created in the likeness of God, is indeed thrown into relief by the fact that we find Christ in every neighbor. But this clearly *presupposes* direct love for Christ Himself (who in His Sacred Humanity is infinitely lovable) as the basis of the love of neighbor.[16]

Charity is impossible without the direct love of God in and through Christ, without the *I-Thou* communion with Christ. This cannot be emphasized enough. Only in this *I-Thou* relationship with Jesus Christ can charity arise in our soul. This is most manifest in the saints. The moment we believe that love of neighbor is the only way to love God, we replace charity in all its glorious and sublime holiness with a mere humanitarian love of neighbor, which in reality can scarcely be called love, but only a pale benevolence.

It would be similarly perverse to claim that the verse in St. John ("He who says, 'I love God,' and hates his brother is a liar"[17]) means that one loves God simply by loving one's neighbor.

[16] In his admirable book *Le paysan de la Garonne* (Paris: Desclée De Brouwer, 1966), 343, Jacques Maritain says that the formula "to see Christ in our brothers" is an abridgement which can easily lead to misunderstandings.

[17] 1 John 4:20.

Love of neighbor tests our love of God

The truth is that the love of neighbor is here a test of our true love of God in and through Christ. This test implies two truths: first, that love of neighbor is a necessary consequence of love of God; second, that love of neighbor is rooted in love of Christ and thus necessarily presupposes it. The relationship here is analogous to that between our love for a person and our corresponding deeds toward him. The latter are obviously a test of our love for him. Thus, we might paraphrase St. John and say that he who claims to love a friend and does not care for his needs is a liar. The absence of good deeds is correctly interpreted as a sign that we do not really love, for deeds are the test of love. But it would be quite wrong to say that the presence of good deeds is not only the *test* for love, but also an adequate *substitute* for love, as if the beneficial deeds were simply equal to love, instead of flowing from it and giving testimony to its presence.

Natural goods deserve our love

The legitimate fear among pious Catholics of an inordinate attachment to finite goods has often led to a suspicious attitude toward all natural goods. This is yet another instance of the working of an incomplete truth. It is certainly good and necessary to be alert to the danger of falling into a disordered attachment; but it is also a most regrettable mistake, propagated at various times in many sermons and religious textbooks, to overlook or underestimate the high values of certain natural goods. An unfortunate penetration of Christian doctrine by a Stoic or over-ascetic spirit caused many Christians to see in every natural good (such as human love, marriage, culture, art, or science) a mere threat of a disordered attachment to a creature. They failed to perceive that the intrinsic value of natural goods contains a message of God, a reflection of His infinite glory. On the condition always that our approach to them is transformed by Christ, that the message of God in them is perceived, that they move us to lift up our hearts to God in gratitude, delight in these goods has a positive value.

Supernatural goods are greater than natural ones

But the negative approach often found in former times to natural goods has evoked a reaction among progressive Catholics which, unfortunately, is not the completion called for by the incomplete truth. On the contrary, it is a wholehearted turning to natural goods that obscures the infinite superiority of supernatural goods and thereby tends to divert us from God.[18]

Natural goods must be loved "in Christ"

The necessity of approaching all natural goods in Christ is also deplorably misunderstood. In a typical case of a false reaction instead of a completion, a crude naturalism has replaced the over-ascetic supernaturalism. This is obviously much worse than the former narrowness, for it denies the achieved truth and introduces grave error.

The *instaurare omnia in Christo* is by no means intended to blur the distinction between the world of the supernatural and the world of even the most sublime created goods. Rather, it implies, on the one hand, a specific recognition of the absolute superiority of the supernatural glory that we find in the Sacred Humanity of Christ and in all the saints to all natural beauty and goodness. On

[18] Cf. Pierre Teilhard de Chardin, *The Divine Milieu* (New York: Harper, 1960), 35: "Everything is sacred."

the other hand, the perception of this superiority should not make us less sensitive to the great values of created goods. It should enable us, rather, to seize on their deepest meaning, as did St. Francis of Assisi in his profound response to the beauty of nature.

Natural goods differ essentially from worldly goods

But not only do progressive Catholics introduce an unchristian naturalism. In their failure to distinguish between high natural goods and worldly goods they fall prey to an utter secularism. In the Liturgy we find the following prayer: May we learn "to despise earthly things and love those of heaven" (*despicere terrena, caelestia desiderare*). This despising of earthly goods has often been wrongly applied to all natural goods, instead of only to worldly goods.[19]

This was certainly a regrettable confusion which called for correction, but those who loudly summon us to get out of the so-called ghetto fail to make the necessary distinction between natural and worldly goods quite as much as did the representatives of over-asceticism. For while the latter extended this suspicion of worldly goods to all natural goods, the former ascribe the value of high natural goods to worldly goods as well. Their secularism fails to attain even the level of pre-Christian, pagan insight.

The drift of the Catholic progressives reaches its ugly climax when they extend their enthusiasm to things which not only are worldly, but embody a blatant disvalue in their absurdity, vulgarity, and impurity — such as the infantile abandon in contemporary dancing.

[19] See Dietrich von Hildebrand, *Not as the World Gives* (Chicago: Franciscan Herald Press, 1963), 71; *The Heart* (Chicago: Franciscan Herald Press, 1977), 175.

Human loves can be compatible with holiness

It is true that there have often entered into the Catholic orbit ideas which had their source in an oriental or Stoic mentality rather than in the teaching of Christ. One example of this is the notion that any love for a creature, apart from the specifically commanded Christian love of neighbor, is incompatible with religious perfection.

Valuable as is the preoccupation with avoiding anything that could sever us from the love of God, it is wrong to believe that filial love, parental love, spousal love, or friendship are incompatible with religious perfection.

Given that our love for creatures is an *amare in Deo* (a love in God), that it is transformed in Christ (without thereby in any way losing its character), there is no incompatibility whatever between these modes of love and religious perfection. St. Augustine's love for St. Monica certainly did not diminish his love for God, nor did the ardent love of St. Louis of France for his wife, Marguerite, diminish his holiness. Rather, these instances of human love, transformed as they were in Christ, gave specific testimony to the holiness of the lovers.

Human loves must be transformed in Christ

Again we witness a false reaction on the part of progressive Catholics. They rightly oppose mistaken asceticism, but overlook the necessity of an *amare in Deo*, the great task of transforming natural loves in Christ. They fail to grasp the great truth that only such transformation brings about the most authentic fulfillment of the intention rooted in the very nature of these various loves of creatures. Further, the progressive Catholics no longer see the danger of a diversion of our hearts from God. Worse, they no longer see the great, absolute primacy of the love of Christ. Instead of the called-for correction that would stress the *amare in Deo*, they deny that human love could raise any problem for a Christian and so they fall into a pagan naturalism.

Holy friendship differs from comradeship

In the past, hypersensitivity to the possibility of conflict between love of creatures (apart from Christian love of neighbor) and religious perfection gained such wide acceptance that the constitutions of many religious orders forbid friendship between their members. But the lives of the saints have something different to say. The Liturgy refers to the last visit of St. Benedict to his sister, St. Scholastica: "She made a request of the Lord, and it carried more weight because she loved more."

Since the love referred to is the love she has for her brother, it clearly shows that love for a creature, when having the character of an *amare in Deo*, is not considered an obstacle to one's total self-donation to God.

But progressive Catholics not only defend the goodness of friendships among members of a religious order; they also believe them entitled to superficial comradeship. They fail to see the incompatibility of superficial chumminess with the sacred atmosphere of a religious order, the members of which have accepted the call to live in the depth and to donate themselves totally to Christ.

Instead of correcting the former narrowness by accenting the difference between a holy friendship in Christ and a mere natural comradeship (and thus showing that whereas the latter really is incompatible with the religious life, the former is entirely compatible with it), the progressives in their reaction lose their sense of the difference between sacred and profane and open the door for secularization of religious life.

Authority has sometimes been abused in the Church

There certainly were many abuses of authority in religious orders and seminaries which led to a depersonalization of religious life and sometimes even to a blunting of conscience. By making formal obedience the most important virtue, by blurring the essential difference between moral virtues and mere disciplinary correctness, by overemphasizing things which, because of their lack of real importance, were trivial, those in authority produced a state of affairs in which the personality of the religious or seminarian was in danger of being emptied and in which the sense of the hierarchy of values was almost inevitably deadened. Narrowness, anxiety, and sometimes mental disturbances were the result. But the Second Vatican Council wrought a great liberation in this area.

Authority and obedience are nonetheless valuable

Now, in reacting — in this case to an abuse of valid principles rather than to an incomplete truth — the progressive Catholics fail to understand the true intentions of the Council and the proper correction of these abuses. Theirs is the classical mistake with regard to an abuse: to lose sight of the value of the thing abused and attempt to do away with it completely. If something is evil, one cannot abuse it. The disvalue of any abuse presupposes that the thing abused has a value. When the abuse of authority and obedience includes a falsification of the nature of these principles, the elimination of the abuse should therefore clarify the sublime value of true obedience and true religious authority.

Pettiness and authoritarian violence are incompatible with the sacred, loving authority of the Abbot or superior in a religious order or seminary. They are incompatible with respect for a human soul, with the generosity and magnanimity which allows the superior to distinguish clearly the essential from the unessential. But the solution of the progressive Catholics is to do away with sacred authority and holy obedience and replace them with a merely technical authority and profane loyalty. They fail to grasp the meaning and beauty of holy obedience, the inner freedom which it bestows on the obedient, the glorious self-donation it implies.[20]

Secularization will not remedy abuse of authority

The recently founded priests' union,[21] though an extreme case, is symptomatic of the misunderstanding of the spirit of the Council. It is believed that the members of the priesthood should follow the lead of most other professions and combine into a union in order to defend their interests against the religious authority of the bishops. But if secularization is the way to overcome narrowness and authoritarian abuses in religious orders, seminaries, and the hierarchy of the Church, if the priesthood is looked upon as a *profession* like that of a physician, a lawyer, or a teacher, and not as a *vocation*, then why should religious orders continue to exist? Why should the vow of obedience be made at all?

In truth, secularization is not the way to overcome abuses that happen to be found in religious orders and in the administration of some dioceses. The secularization recommended by some progressive Catholics would rather undermine the *raison d'être* of religious orders and of dioceses. The true way to overcome these

20 In "The Woman Intellectual and the Church," *Commonweal* 85, (1966-67): 446-58, it is obvious that holy obedience is interpreted as "submissiveness" in the pejorative sense of the term.

21 We refer to the organization founded by Fr. Du Bay of the diocese of Los Angeles.

abuses, on the other hand, is clearly stated in the marvelous "Declaration on Religious Freedom" promulgated by the Second Vatican Council.[22]

Religious coercion is not licit

This "Declaration on Religious Freedom" declares that all types of coercion in religious matters are incompatible with the spirit of Christ. It is an elementary human temptation continually arising in history to try to draw other persons into the Church by force — either out of a domineering spirit or real love — if this is not possible by other means. But every coercion in this area is not only an infringement on the most elementary of human rights; the use of force and pressure, successful as it may be in the legal sphere and in any training, can never lead to true conversion. The Apostles never used force and pressure in their apostolate. And in the fourth century, St. Martin of Tours traveled from Tours to Trier to implore the emperor not to use force of arms against Arianism.

Yet evangelization remains a duty

Unfortunately, however, the Council's condemnation of coercion is being interpreted by many progressive Catholics as an invitation to cease to burn for the conversion of non-Catholics. They believe that we should approach non-Catholics without working — or even without hoping — for their conversion. They have forgotten that every Catholic who really believes that the divine revelation of Christ has been entrusted to the Church and that She has preserved this truth through Her infallible magisterium cannot but see in every non-Catholic a catechumen in

22 *Dignitatis Humanae.*

hope. They consider this presumption, intolerance, disrespect for the freedom of other persons, and "triumphalism." They see pluralism as a sign of intellectual vitality. They even go so far as to claim that we should learn about spiritual matters from atheists.

This is a complete distortion of the great and wonderful message of the Council. It replaces the violent impetuosity of coercion, not with the meekness of a St. Francis de Sales, but with an indifference toward whether or not other persons find the full truth. The negative element that was on occasion attached to a great mission of the Church has led progressive Catholics to throw out the mission itself. Moreover, they equate freedom of conscience from any external coercion or pressure with the absence of an obligation to surrender to the revelation of God in Christ and to convert to His Church.[23]

True science does not contradict revealed truth

The Second Vatican Council adopted a new attitude toward science. Instead of stressing defense of the deposit of Catholic faith against anti-religious interpretations of scientific discoveries, the Council emphasized the value of scientific progress as such. It is indeed a great task to preserve the integrity of revealed truth while doing justice to all genuinely scientific discoveries. A real contradiction between revealed truth and science can never exist. Not

[23] "To everyone should be guaranteed the possibility of seeking truth in a personal way, whether the result will be the Christian God or any other interpretation of existence. This freedom naturally also allows one to be concerned with Jesus Christ and to accept His ideas, if one considers them to be good. But it should permit likewise the rejection of Jesus and the adoption of other ideas." *Monatszeitschrift der Jungenschaft im Bund der Deutschen Katholischen Jugend* (July-August, 1965). As quoted in Bishop Rudolf Graber's book, *Papst Paul VI und die innerkirchliche Krisis* (Zurich: Thomas, 1966), 18.

scientific discoveries themselves, but only wrong philosophical interpretations of them can be incompatible with revealed truth.

Philosophical judgments exceed the authority of science

It is not sufficiently realized that natural scientists often give to their scientific findings a philosophical interpretation which must be clearly distinguished from the conclusions of science as such.

Scientists are frequently not aware of the fact that by their philosophical interpretations they are transcending the limits of science proper. This happens more often in biology than in physics and chemistry. The notion of evolution, for example, has concealed diverse philosophical premises. And when it comes to sociology, psychology, and psychiatry, the role of philosophy goes much further. Here, the intrusion of philosophical assumptions and inferences is not extrinsic to the practice of the science, as is the case in physics, or chemistry, or biology; rather, certain philosophical theories are intimately involved at the very beginning of the scientific work. All attempts on the part of such "scientists" to deny this and to present their work as a natural science are founded on gross self-deception.

The philosophical presuppositions of the starting point of a scientific exploration can be incompatible with revealed truth. If so, it is because they are wrong. They have not been proved by strictly scientific methods as sociologists and psychologists often claim. Marxism, for example, is not the result of mere sociological exploration, but is based on a radically mistaken philosophy.

The work of disentangling the conclusions and observations of science from philosophical presuppositions and interpretations has become much more urgent in our time than it ever was before. This is an important mission for Catholic philosophers and theologians.

In performing it, they will make it clear that all contradictions between scientific discoveries and revealed truth are only apparent. But the very basis for the fruitful accomplishment of this task is an unshakable faith in revealed truth and a firm understanding of its incomparable primacy.

Legitimate and illegitimate forms of scriptural exegesis

This general problem has its application to scriptural exegesis. Here, too, we must distinguish different aspects of the practical effort.

First, there is a *scientific exegesis* based on philological historical research which attempts to determine the accuracy of translations and texts, the chronology of the different Gospels, the authenticity of parts of the Old Testament, and the like. Second, there is an *exegetical criticism* which is based on philosophical presuppositions. The evaluation of the historical authenticity of parts of the Gospels is inevitably dependent upon one's philosophical point of view. Third, there is a specifically *religious exegesis* which deals, for example, with the meaning of the parables, which delves into the inexhaustible plenitude of the words of Christ.

The first is a real scientific work. Like all historical and philological exploration, this can progress in time. It has, moreover, the character of all strictly scientific undertakings in that it admits and even demands teamwork.

But the second is not in the same sense strictly scientific. If one doubts the authenticity of the miracles of the Lord, philosophical views obviously play a decisive role in one's doubts. If one asserts that we cannot expect a modern man to believe in the corporeal apparition of the Angel Gabriel at the Annunciation, one's position is obviously not supported by the first kind of strictly scientific exegesis.

Belief in the improbability — if not in the impossibility — of miracles is not based on scientific findings but on certain philosophical presuppositions. Therefore, there is the constant danger that wrong philosophical views, as well as pervasive contemporary prejudices, may interfere with a man's ability to discern historical authenticity.

The third type of exegesis is not at all of a scientific order. The value of religious interpretations depends upon the genius of the individual theologian, and especially upon his religious depth and charisma. The interpretation of a Father of the Church, of a saint or a mystic, has much more interest and weight than that of professors of exegesis. A deeper penetration of the unfathomable depth of our Lord's parables and sayings is not guaranteed by scientific studies, but by the religious intuition of an individual person, as submitted always to the endorsement of the infallible magisterium of the Church.[24] This third aspect of exegesis, like other branches of theology, is thus not scientific even to the moderate extent of the second. It requires men who are at least *homines religiosi* (religious men) and not mere professors.

The proper role of scientific scriptural exegesis

Now, the change called for in our time has to do only with the first kind of strictly philosophical scientific exegesis. In what concerns the second (or philosophical) kind, an *aggiornamento* (modernization) is obviously not in question. The intellectual climate of our epoch is such that it menaces a sound approach to the miracles and supernatural events in the Gospel. To appreciate

[24] Hans Urs von Balthasar has made the illuminating observation that before the Council of Trent (1545-1563) the great theologians were mostly saints and mystics, whereas after this Council theology and mysticism parted.

the nature of this menace we need consider only the fetish that is made of natural science, the historical relativism so widespread among philosophers, all the attacks on the real meaning of truth, and the confusion between myth and religion in the Bultmannian fad of demythologization.[25] Nor can the notion of *aggiornamento* be applied to the third (or religious) kind of exegesis. A great *homo religiosus*, a saint and mystic endowed with the gift of interpretation, can appear in any and every epoch of history, and the value of his exegesis is completely independent of the course of history.

But all this has been forgotten by the progressive Catholics who have radically misinterpreted the openness manifested by the Council to science and scientific accomplishments in all fields. They believe, rather, that scriptural exegesis and Church doctrine should be adapted to contemporary "scientific" discoveries or to "sociological" and "psychological" theories which in reality conceal shallow and downright fallacious philosophies wrongly presented as the results of scientific research.

Wrong forms of scriptural exegesis

Armed with slogans about the necessity of adapting to the scientific mentality or to "the epoch in which man has come of age," the progressives propose changes in the very dogma of the Church. This is seen, for example, in their attempt to deny the historical reality of the miracles related in the Gospels, and even the historical reality of the essential mysteries of the Annunciation and the Resurrection.[26]

[25] Theologian Rudolf Bultmann (1884-1976).

[26] Cf., for example, Gregorius Rhenanus, *Aufbruch oder Zusammenbruch?* (Zurich: Thomas, 1966). On page 7 of this work, the author says of Father Paulus Gordan's article on the Resurrection: "While reading this article it

Let us consider the argument of some Catholic exegetes who claim that the passage in the Gospel of St. Matthew ("Thou art the Christ, Son of the living God . . . "[27]) cannot be authentic, because if St. Peter had really believed that Jesus was the Son of God, he would not have denied Him.

This argument obviously has nothing whatever to do with science. It amounts to no more than psychological guesswork, which is moreover superficial psychology and naive guesswork. To believe that man is consistent in all his behavior is to ignore human frailty. Even a man who has an absolute faith in Christ can deny Him on innumerable occasions. Our daily lives teach us how easily we contradict our faith in our actions. Does the fact of a man's genuine faith guarantee that he will be ready to die a martyr?

Furthermore, St. Peter's denial is a typical case of the tragedy of immanent logic. His resolution to remain unknown so that he could follow Jesus and see what happened to Him led him to succumb to the immanent logic dictated by this resolution. It is a classical example of man's frailty and discloses in a unique way man's tragic situation, which consists precisely in the mysterious contradiction between the greatest love, the firmest faith, and one's behavior. What would Dostoyevsky or Kierkegaard have said of the psychology which produced so shallow an exegesis?

Surely, before Pentecost St. Peter did not clearly understand that Christ was called to redeem mankind by His death on the Cross. He chided the Lord when He predicted His passion and death. So it is understandable that despite his firm belief that Jesus was the Christ, Son of the living God, St. Peter was confused and frightened at the moment of Jesus' condemnation.

is impossible to know whether the Resurrection of Christ or only the belief in it is an historical fact."

[27] Matt. 16:16.

No one can honestly claim that the commentary we have examined deserves the name of science or that it should have any bearing on our acceptance of the authenticity of the passage from St. Matthew.[28] It is further evidence of the drastic contrast between the decrees of the Council and the articles and books by progressive Catholics who would inundate the Church with secularism. We shall return to the question of phony *aggiornamento* and pseudo-science — especially when we examine the science fetishism characteristic of our epoch.

[28] We are, of course, prescinding here from the problem of the meaning of the titles of Christ in the Lucan and Marcan parallels as it bears on the confession of Peter in Matthew 16.

5

Vivification of religion

ONE OF THE GREAT PURPOSES of Vatican II was to vivify the religious life of the faithful, to permeate their lives with the Christian revelation. Without any doubt, legalistic, formalistic trends have often appeared in the Church, veiling the light of Christ and the glorious reality of Holy Church.

Ossification threatens every institution

Of course, the danger of such ossification is always present in every institution. Even if the institution is, like the Church, a supernatural one, the human persons in it are not exempt from this danger. As we have indicated, the eternal, supernatural vitality of the Church manifests itself throughout Her history precisely in the fact that these tendencies to ossification have always been overcome through a continual renewal.

In order to clarify the nature of the renewal required today, we shall discuss briefly several examples of a legalistic and formalistic approach. This attitude is, in fact, naturalistic because it derives from regarding the Church as a merely human institution and loses sight — at least in practice — of Her supernatural character.

A neutral attitude cripples catechesis

Religion has often been taught to children in the same way as history or spelling. Instead of presenting the mysteries of Christian faith in a way proper to their unique and extraordinary character, teachers of religion have often taught them with a kind of neutral objectivity suitable to any purely academic matter.

The real teacher of religion, on the contrary, communicates the realization that religion is something completely different from any other topic. He appeals to the entire person. He creates a truly religious atmosphere which evokes feelings of wonder and awe in the child and at the same time corresponds to the longing for God that lives in every human soul. The real teacher of religion attempts to awaken and develop a sense of mystery and reverence in his pupil.

Religious truth, which appeals to faith, cannot be taught in the manner of secular subjects which appeal either to a mere apprehension or to a rational understanding. To teach religion as just one topic of learning among others (as is currently being recommended to the public schools of the United States) is one example of the neutralization of religion which renders it dull and inert and incapable of penetrating our entire life.

Loyalty to the Church is not the same as faith

Another example is the tendency to substitute for real faith a mere loyalty to the Church as an organization with rules for its members. Instead of being aware of the awful privilege of assisting at Holy Mass, many Catholics go to church on Sunday just as they fulfill profane duties out of loyalty to the country or to an institution to which they belong. That is, they perform this task because they just happen to be Catholics. Here, indeed, the letter has replaced the spirit. This substitution of loyalty for holy obedience and grateful love indicates the loss of a true understanding of the nature of the Church. It suggests that the Church is a merely human institution.

I remember how often, during the first persecutions of the Jews from 1933 to 1936, Catholics could be heard saying that as long as Hitler did not attack the Church, he could not be called an enemy of the Church. These persons did not understand that the Church was attacked each time God was offended by an injustice. They had become blind to the universality of the Church. They had forgotten the words of Pope Benedict XV who said that he was the father of all, whether they wanted to accept it or not, whether they knew it or not. They had forgotten that St. Ambrose refused to let the Emperor Theodosius into church because he had killed six thousand innocent persons in Samos. St. Ambrose did not ask whether those murdered innocents were Catholics or not.

The consideration of the Church as a state or, even worse, as a political party could indeed be called a Catholic ghetto mentality. This outlook fails to see that unlike all natural institutions, the Church has no other interests than those of God.

Bureaucratic attitudes stifle faith

Still another example of dried-up religion is a phenomenon one could well call *employeeism*. Instead of emanating a spirit of holy unction, of loving zeal for the glorification of God and for guiding the faithful to Christ, priests have sometimes behaved as if they were employees of the Church. The way they say Mass suggests the performance of a professional duty. Their contact with the faithful is similar to that of an organization official dealing with clients.

In contrast to the priest who leads an immoral life or who is immersed in worldly preoccupations — a danger widespread in the Renaissance — these employee-priests who have taken the letter for the spirit do not have a bad conscience. They feel themselves to be very correct and loyal. This makes their attitude, though not sinful as the other is, very dangerous to the life of the Church. They not only tend to reduce their own religious life to correctness and loyalty; they also influence the faithful to take such an approach.

I remember a sermon by a Dominican on the vigil of St. Sylvester. "The main question we should pose in our examination of conscience at the end of the year," he said, "should be, 'How often have we received the sacrament of the Eucharist?' "

Such a ritualistic conception of one's religious life leaves no place for transformation in Christ — a process that implies orienting one's entire life around Christ and bearing witness to Christ in one's contact with the world. But many Catholics, having accepted the Catholic faith as a mere heritage similar to their nationality, having failed ever to come to a full profession of faith, to an awareness of what it means to be a member of the Mystical Body of Christ, are completely lost and helpless when confronted with atheists.

They yield, or at least remain silent, when atheists say something incompatible with Christian revelation or that betrays an ignorance of the Church. They are silent because they consider Catholicism to be something only for Catholics, for those who belong to it, as they belong to family or country. It therefore does not apply or refer to "outsiders." These Catholics have made a mere ghetto of the all-embracing Church which addresses Herself to every human being with the good tidings of the Gospel.

Organizations can never replace personal commitment

A widespread symptom of a formalistic or legalistic religion is overestimation of organization. Full personal commitment, as well as immediate contact from person to person, is being more and more replaced by organizations. The efficiency of organizations in the life of civilization — in activities of a social, practical order — has created the illusion that this more mechanized, impersonal way of dealing with problems is just what religious life needs. And yet, in religion everything depends upon personal contact.

A typical example of this illusion is the way many interpreted the original idea of Catholic Action as set forth by Pope Pius XI in his Encyclical *Pax Christi in Regno Christi*. The Pope called for penetration of the entire life of the layman by the spirit of Christ and for a new participation of laymen in the apostolate. This sublime call to full personal commitment was interpreted by many as a summons to mere organizational activity — as if the main task was to establish a headquarters for all Catholic associations.

The overestimation of organization as such found its purest expression in the words of a famous German Archbishop who went so far as to exclaim, "The Catholic associations are the eighth sacrament of the Church." The depersonalization of religious activity that this spirit brought about is obviously closely related to the aforementioned employeeism

To see the enormous difference between a total commitment of the individual person and the activities of religious associations, we need only compare the conversion of the residents of the outskirts of Paris with the work of any Catholic charitable association. Pierre Lhande tells of the Italian priest who first went to the people there who were living like animals in an indescribable poverty, in promiscuity, and in a ferocious hatred of Christ and His Holy Church. When this priest arrived, a youngster, seeing the cassock, hit him in the head so hard with a stone that the blood ran down his face. The priest picked up the stone and said, "Thank you, my boy. This will be the cornerstone of my church." This example of heroic devotion, of answering every offense with inexhaustible patience and love and with a willingness to accept all humiliations, opened the door for the apostolate. Several Paris pastors joined this priest, and Catholic students came one day every week to live with these workers and help them. After twenty years of this personal apostolate, a full third of all vocations to the priesthood in Paris came from this area.[29]

Religious naturalism leads to formalism and legalism

The cause of formalism and legalism consists precisely in approaching supernatural truth through natural categories. Even though the supernatural was stressed in the abstract, those responsible for ossification in the Church retained a way of thinking and acting that was secular. The moment they left the abstract plane, their approach to religion breathed only a secular atmosphere which could not sustain authentic Christian revelation. Absent was the breath of Christ, the epiphany of God; absent was the perfume of holiness, the splendor of the supernatural, all so gloriously present in the saints and *homines religiosi* to whom we have referred. This lack drains life from religion, creates a Catholic ghetto, and deprives the message of Christ of its irresistible power.

Revitalization requires emphasis on the supernatural

It is against the background of a legalistic and formalistic conception of religion, then, that we must see the appeal of

[29] Pierre Lhande, S.J., *Le Christ dans la banlieue* (Paris: Plon, 1927).

Vatican II for a vivification of our religion. Father Lombardi wrote of this even before the Council started. One of the things he said the Council should achieve was to make the bishops less administrators than fathers of their dioceses.

It is difficult to understand how the vivification of religion can be sought in a secularization of religion, as the progressive Catholics advocate. If religion is to penetrate our lives, the primary requisite is that it be itself authentic religion. The first step toward vivification, therefore, is to replace mere learning with a discovery of the glory of Christian faith. The Church must be recognized as the Mystical Body of Christ and profane loyalty must be replaced with holy obedience and the ardent love of the Church. Moreover, instead of concentrating exclusively and maliciously on the narrowness and legalism that have appeared in the Church over the last centuries, one should rather call attention to the host of saints and great religious personalities which blossomed during this period. They are the pattern of true vitality, the very opposite of the inhabitants of a Catholic ghetto. Their example reveals how to overcome the arid, formalistic, legalistic tendencies that ossify religion. To think of a Don Bosco, a Lacordaire, or a Newman is to discern the path leading to true vivification.

True vivification requires that the supernatural spirit of Christ be fully thrown into relief. This means eliminating any blurring of the distinction between the natural and the supernatural. Yet the progressive Catholics opt for more blurring. They believe that vivification can come to pass through secularization. They want to increase the thrust of natural categories. They thus advocate a cure that was the very cause of the formalism of religious life in the past. In calling for a full and deliberate secularization, they recommend worldly activism and bohemian freedom. They forget that what was wrong with the dried-up, formalistic approach that stressed the letter over the spirit was precisely that the Holy Spirit was screened out by abstraction and by too great a concession to purely natural methods.

Secularization suffocates religion

The victory of Christ in every domain of life is the real end. Yet we bury the Christian faith and Christian life when we attempt to overcome the sterility of a legalistic religion by turning from the spirit of Christ to the *saeculum*, by substituting for the holy fire of Christ a secular enthusiasm, by forgetting the supernatural vitality of the saints and embracing the nervous, hectic, profane preoccupations of the modern world.

It is easy to feel oneself alive and free if one forgets about the *unum necessarium*, the one thing necessary, and directs all one's powers toward secular endeavors. It is easy to feel oneself bursting with energy if, for example, the clearance of slums concerns one more than transformation in Christ. What the progressives call "leaving the Catholic ghetto" is in reality giving up the Catholic and keeping the ghetto. They would replace the universal Church with the ghetto of secularism, with imprisonment in a stifling immanentism, with isolation in a world that sits *in umbra mortis*, in the shadow of death.[30] To achieve a unity of religion and life by adapting religion to the *saeculum* does not result in a union of religion with our daily life, but reduces religion to the pursuit of purely mundane goals.[31]

It must certainly be admitted that priests have, at times, scandalized people because of their religious mediocrity. Oftentimes, they were harmless bourgeois whose personalities never breathed

30 Ps. 22:4 (RSV = Ps. 23:4).

31 In reading Daniel Callahan, for example, one gets the impression that the clearance of slums should have precedence over redemption.

a religious atmosphere. Sometimes they were filled with suspicion against every sort of *élan*. They oversimplified all questions. They were incapable of understanding the message of God contained in great art and in other great natural works of man.

These were regrettable features, indeed, of the practical life of the Church. But the way to overcome them is certainly not to encourage priests to fall into another extreme by abandoning their former narrowness for indiscriminate ravings about secular crudities or for a taste insensitive to vulgarity. This is to flee from one mediocrity to another. The progressives tend to believe that narrowness is the only kind of mediocrity. They forget that being blind to those things which are antagonistic to true greatness and true culture and lavishing enthusiasm on shallow worldliness are expressions of a more blatant mediocrity and are even more incompatible with religion.[32]

The fallacy in the progressivist approach is obvious. If we assert that religion should permeate our lives, the implication is that we should break through to the realization of the primary vocation, the very meaning of our lives, which is our re-creation in Christ. We should then no longer be exclusively absorbed by the immanent logic of our professional lives or by everyday preoccupations, but should see them and all things in the light of Christ. Indeed, the echo of our self-donation to Christ should resound through all the scenes of our lives.

Efficiency is not holiness

It is the very opposite of uniting true religion with everyday life to believe that all that is demanded from a Christian is to fulfill

[32] We are thinking of the attempt to introduce jazz or rock and roll into religious services.

the duties prescribed by the logic of his secular life. This would mean the absorption of religion by secular activities, so that we would be satisfied that in fulfilling the requirements of these we were doing everything that God could ask of us. In reality this is to avoid the confrontation with Christ. Those who act in this way are Christians in name only.

The decisive question for the vivification of religion today is whether through the light of Christ our everyday lives will become deeply changed and adapted to Him, or whether the Christian religion is to be adapted to the immanent logic of mundane concerns.

The mistaken approach to uniting the Christian religion with the whole of our life promotes efficiency over holiness. We have dealt with this confusion in *The New Tower of Babel*.[33] This error, which marks the proposals of Daniel Callahan and others, betrays the loss of the *sensus supranaturalis*. The quality of holiness and the self-revelation of God in Christ are simply not seen or, if seen, misunderstood and downgraded. The ideal of these progressive reformers seems to be that instead of aiming at a transformation in Christ and being a witness to the Christian revelation, a Catholic should be as little as possible distinguishable from a humanitarian philanthropist.

[33] Chicago: Franciscan Herald Press, 1977.

6

Christian revelation and philosophy

THERE IS a growing confusion among Catholics today concerning the nature of the relationship between Christian revelation (and, consequently, the Catholic Church) and philosophy.

The Church cannot employ false philosophies

Before the Second Vatican Council many Catholics were convinced that in order to be an orthodox Catholic, it was necessary also to be a Thomist. Now, after the Council, many believe that in order to be up to date, the Church must sever its connection with Thomism (which has been especially strong since the Council of Trent) and ally Herself with a radically different philosophy, such as Heideggerian existentialism or Hegelianism.

This attitude implies that the relation between Christian revelation and philosophy has hitherto been accidental. It assumes that only historical influences caused the Church to associate herself first with Platonic and later with Aristotelian philosophy. This naive oversimplification has entailed great confusion.

There can be no doubt that there is an essential relation between Christian revelation and certain fundamental natural truths. The existence of objective truth, the spiritual reality of the person, the difference between soul and body, the objectivity of moral good and evil, the freedom of the will, the immortality of the soul, the existence of a personal God — all are implied by Christian revelation. Every word in the New Testament clearly presupposes these elementary truths. And any philosophy that denies them can never be accepted or tolerated by the Church.

To be sure, a genuine Christian faith does not imply a philosophical grasp of these truths, still less a philosophical formulation of them. But true faith constitutes an implicit acceptance of these basic natural truths and therefore categorically excludes any philosophy that denies them. The very nature of the Judaeo-Christian revelation makes for an absolute incompatibility with any epistemological, metaphysical, or moral relativism, with any materialism, immanentism, subjectivism, or determinism, to say nothing of atheism.

Thus, while the connection between Christian revelation and the fundamental truths we have enumerated must be distinguished both from the role a given philosophy or philosophical system plays in the teaching of the Church and from the influence a given philosophy has on theological speculations, we can never speak of the Church's choice of a certain philosophy as having been historically conditioned insofar as these elementary natural truths are concerned.

Philosophy for the Church must be adequate to revelation

But the relation between Christian revelation and philosophy is not exhausted by the fact that every philosophy denying these essential truths is incompatible with the deposit of the Catholic faith, for the philosophies that acknowledge them vary widely in their adequacy to the demands of Christian revelation. Whatever agreement there may be on these basic truths, a philosophy that does more justice than others to the plenitude of being will for this very reason be better fitted to explain, for example, the relation of natural to Christian morality. Again, a philosophy that delves more deeply into the nature of the person will contribute more to the study of the meaning of man's being created in the likeness of God or of the mystery of the two natures of the one person of Christ. In these cases one can say that such a philosophy corresponds more adequately to revealed truth.

Thus, there can be completely adequate reasons for the Church to favor one philosophy over others that equally accept the basic truths that are from the beginning necessarily presupposed and implied by Christian revelation. And these reasons are quite independent of mere historical influence. There should be freedom in the discussion of all philosophical questions. But as long as the indispensable presuppositions are guaranteed, it is quite possible that the specific content of one philosophical conception will be more in harmony with revealed truth than another and will be explicitly appropriated by the Church for this very reason. In the next chapter we shall consider further the relative adequacy to reality of various philosophies — that is, the goal of philosophy considered in itself, rather than in relation to revealed truth. Needless to say, for all who are convinced Catholics these two approaches must inevitably and objectively converge, though they are formally distinct.

The Church avoids philosophies open to misinterpretation

In addition to the recognition of certain basic truths and the suitability for the study of the meaning of revealed truth, there is a third factor that plays a role in the Church's sponsorship of a particular philosophy. Though one philosophy may be deeper and superior in truth and thus objectively more adequate than another to Christian revelation, it may lend itself more to misinterpretation and so may pose more pedagogical risks.

Preference for a closed system, such as Thomism, is certainly motivated — at least in part — by the fact that it protects the mind from philosophical adventures that may lead to heresies. The Augustinian philosophical tradition in St. Anselm and St. Bonaventure is certainly not less adequate to Christian revelation than Thomistic philosophy. But it does not have the character of a closed system. Its openness is a decided advantage from a purely philosophical point of view, but pedagogically it can be dangerous. A closed system recommends itself as the philosophical basis for the education of priests and as the material with which to build a theological fortress against possible heretical deviations.

Now, we do not by any means claim that these three factors in the relation between the doctrine of the Church and philosophy are the only ones. But they should suffice to show that the Church cannot arbitrarily exchange one philosophy for another merely because of historical influences.

Historical factors cannot explain the Church's philosophy

Nor do we deny that historical influences also play a role in the Church's endorsement of a particular philosophy. The intrusion of an Averroistic Aristotelianism into the Christian world at the beginning of the thirteenth century, for example, certainly played a role in the ascendancy of Thomism over the Augustinian tradition, but this was by no means the only reason.

It is a disastrous error to hold that any philosophy could ever be accepted by the Church because of the historical situation and without regard for its inner affinity with Christian revelation. Today it is necessary to stress this point: no matter what the intellectual climate happens to be in the course of history, no philosophy that denies the fundamental natural truths essentially presupposed by Christian revelation could ever be accepted or even tolerated by the Church.

The role of Plato's philosophy in the writings of the Fathers of the Church was certainly not due merely to historical influence. It was based primarily upon the fact that the truths we have mentioned were either acknowledged or tacitly assumed. They were never formally denied. It would have been impossible to accept other Greek philosophies, such as Sophism, the Skepticism of the later Academies, or Stoicism. Nor could Thomistic Aristotelianism ever have been able to play such a significant role in the later Middle Ages if it could not have been shown that Aristotle's philosophy had more or less acknowledged these same basic truths. This is best seen in the fact that the Church endorsed St. Thomas's interpretation of Aristotle and condemned the Averroistic one.

Plato's importance in patristic times and the earlier Middle Ages is also explained by the second factor in the relation between the Church and philosophy. The high philosophical rank of this philosophy gave it an inner affinity with Christian revelation. The noble ring of Platonism, the role it assigns to contemplation, the deep reverence that pervades it, and its upward gaze — these qualities strongly recommended Plato to those who were seeking a philosophical basis for a theology of Christian doctrine.

The Church's philosophy cannot contradict revelation

It is with the foregoing analysis and examples in mind that we should approach the contemporary discussion of the Church and philosophy.

Many of the progressive Catholics who today call for a new philosophy for the Church seem to have no idea of the real relationship between the truths of the Catholic faith and the philosophy that the Church might recommend as a natural guide to truth and as an aid for theology. The notion of a *new philosophy* contains a perilous ambiguity. It could mean that traditional philosophy ought to be replaced by philosophies which deny the basic natural truths which Christian faith assumes.[34] As we have seen, such a "new" philosophy would in fact be radically incompatible with the Church. Or it could refer to philosophical completions of traditional philosophy, including the replacement of unsatisfactory or shaky arguments.

Now, this latter represents a legitimate endeavor, as long as it is realized that *the weakness of a proof does not suffice to disprove the truth of a thesis*. The fact that philosophers agree on a fundamental truth (such as the difference between body and soul, the possibility of attaining absolute truth, or freedom of the will) is more decisive than their disagreement over arguments on behalf of that truth. In natural theology there is more agreement than disagreement between St. Anselm and St. Thomas. It is more significant that St. Thomas also affirms the existence of God and the possibility of rational knowledge of the existence of God than that he rejects St. Anselm's ontological proof of the existence of God.

Again, the epistemologies of both St. Augustine and of St. Thomas have a place in a philosophy accepted by the Church because both affirm the existence of objective truth and the possibility of attaining objective and absolutely certain knowledge. As long as the philosophical *newness* does not attempt to

[34] Cf. Eugene Fontinell's proposals in *Cross Currents* 16 (1966): 15-40.

undermine the fundamental truths presupposed by Christian revelation and accepted by traditional philosophy, it might well be acceptable to the Church.

There is an analogous relationship between dogma and theology. A theology that denied any article of faith — or even gave it a different interpretation from the traditional one — would necessarily be false. If, for example, the recent changes in the catechism in Holland and France (such as the omission of all mention of Hell) were made, not just for pedagogical reasons, but for the sake of a "new" theology that no longer accepted these revealed truths, this enterprise would obviously be heretical. By the same token, any theology that denied the presence of Christ in the Holy Eucharist after the Consecration would also be heretical. Many theological theories that do not affect the facts of revealed truth can be replaced by others. There is no doubt, for example, that certain theories about predestination are badly in need of reformulation. But the facts revealed to us, which find their expression in dogma, can never be replaced with a "new theology."[35]

[35] Such an attempt at a new theology is clearly made by Leslie Dewart in his book *The Future of Belief* (New York: Herder and Herder, 1966), in which he says that "Christian theism might in the future not conceive God as a person or indeed as a Trinity of persons."

7

The task of the Christian philosopher today

GIVEN THAT divine revelation implies certain fundamental natural truths, a question of some moment must now be raised: What should be the attitude of the Catholic philosopher now that Thomism is no longer universally identified as the only philosophy that properly corresponds to divine revelation? Before we answer this question, however, we must deal with the processes of organic growth in philosophy to which we referred in Chapter 3.

Philosophy begins with direct contact with being

The principal prerequisite for discovering significant philosophical truth is an unprejudiced analysis of the intelligible data of the cosmos. All philosophical discovery begins with genuine wonder and questioning, and demands a readiness to listen to the voice of being in all its intelligible manifestations.[36]

[36] We have discussed this immediate contact with "the given" in *What Is Philosophy?* (London: Routledge, 1991).

It is this contact with being that is manifested in the history of philosophy whenever great insights are achieved, such as Plato's discovery of two different forms of knowledge in the *Meno*, Aristotle's discoveries in logic in his *Organon*, or St. Augustine's distinction between *uti* (use) and *frui* (enjoyment).

Philosophy completes incomplete truths

An intuitive contact with "the given," a constantly renewed consultation of reality, also produces that more modest real growth in philosophical knowledge which occurs each time an incomplete truth finds completion. We must again emphasize that an incomplete truth is in no way an error, nor can it be termed a "relative" truth.

An incomplete truth is as true as a complete truth, even though it still calls for completion. The statement that "the morally good is a value and not merely subjectively satisfying" is true although it is incomplete since it does not indicate the specific nature of moral values or show what distinguishes them from intellectual and aesthetic values. Numerous examples of such incomplete truths can be given, all absolutely true notwithstanding their incompleteness.

The act of completing incomplete truths may take diverse forms. It may appear as a further differentiation, a greater specification, or even the perception of new distinctions within the framework of an already conquered truth. It may take the form of a discovery of another aspect of a being. Sometimes it involves delving deeper into a realm of being and continuing former insights, but seeing heretofore unseen complexities and ramifications. This kind of development can sometimes be found in the lifework of an individual philosopher, as well as in the entire history of philosophy.

Philosophy disentangles truth from errors

A third important process in the growth of philosophy is the disentangling of a formerly discovered truth from errors connected with it. Thus, Plato's great epistemological discovery in the *Meno* is allied to such errors as the pre-existence of the soul. Freeing this great truth from error by showing there is no necessary connection between them would represent a real advance in philosophy. Kant's discovery of the difference between a hypothetical and a categorical obligation and his explicit emphasis on the categorical character of moral obligation is a very important insight, but he linked it with the unfortunate formalism of the categorical imperative and thereby severed all morality from the value on the object side. This case, too, calls for disentangling truth from error.

Philosophy replaces weak arguments with strong ones

A fourth process of growth in philosophy involves replacing weak arguments for an important truth with convincing ones. This is an especially urgent work, for as we have seen, many naively believe that significant insights are false because the arguments that have been advanced in their support are not valid.

Philosophy unmasks fundamental errors

A fifth process consists in the unmasking of fundamental errors that have barred the way to truth throughout the history of philosophy. This is sometimes done by showing the equivocal nature of a term, as Edmund Husserl did when he showed that the term *judgment* simultaneously signifies the personal, conscious act of affirmation and the sentence composed of subject, predicate, and copula — indeed, two radically different entities.

These hints show that growth in attaining philosophical truth is neither automatic nor governed by the rhythm of thesis, antithesis, and synthesis. As we saw, although this rhythm may sometimes be found in the course of history, a synthesis need not by any means be nearer the truth than the preceding "stages" and, in fact, may be even further from the truth.

It is against the background of this analysis that we must pursue the question of the attitude the Catholic philosopher should adopt today. Wrong as it was to remain imprisoned in a strict Thomistic system and fight as error every philosophical thesis that did not fit into this system, bad as it was to believe that all philosophical questions could be answered by Thomism, it is yet much worse to react as do many types of progressive Catholic philosophers.

Some moderns abandon Thomism for relativism

There is first of all the one who, the moment his belief in Thomism as the ultimate word in philosophy is shattered, suffers a traumatic disillusionment. His belief in philosophical truth as such is undermined and he becomes more or less a relativist. Instead of disentangling the great insights of St. Thomas from various imperfections, instead of confronting everything with the plenitude of being and thus completing the discoveries of St. Thomas with new distinctions and new differentiations, he becomes an historical relativist. This is the opposite of greater open-mindedness. This is to ape the man who, having been disappointed in love, now despairs of the possibility of any woman's being faithful.

Some moderns embrace false philosophies

A second type is the man who exchanges his wholesale acceptance of the Thomistic system for an equally wholesale acceptance of a philosophy such as that of Heidegger, Hegel, Kant, or even Freud. Such a man does not despair of the possibility of attaining philosophical truth, but rather yields to a modern system of philosophy with the same uncritical and self-surrendering abandon that possessed him when he occupied the fortress of Thomism.

However, the philosophy to which he gives himself now is a complete error and in its very foundation incompatible with the Christian faith. Instead of doing second-hand thinking based on great Catholic thinkers, he now does second-hand thinking based on mistaken secular thinkers. Apart from the fact that he continues to do second-hand thinking (manifesting thereby a regrettable conservative tendency), the life of his spirit undergoes a profound change. He now seeks shelter in thought that actually tempts him to contradict the truths of divine revelation. One can apply to such a person the words of the Gospel: ". . . and the last state of that man becomes worse than the first."[37]

Some moderns mix Thomism with false philosophies

A third type of contemporary Catholic philosopher believes that he can overcome a narrow Thomism by making a concoction of Thomas and Kant, or Hegel, or some other influential modern thinker. He fails to see that the former narrowness did not result from the content of Thomism, but from the erroneous belief that one can find an answer to everything in the consistency of a closed system. Defense of the system often replaced consultation of reality. The proper remedy is an unprejudiced approach to "the given," not the admixture of another system with Thomism. The reaction of this third type also overlooks the absolute incompatibility of the new ingredients with divine revelation.

[37] Matt. 12:45.

The mission of the modern Catholic philosopher

The proper response of the Catholic philosopher today requires a deeply reverent and organic contact with the great insights of traditional philosophy coupled with the continual consultation of the plenitude of being, as he attempts to complete the great truths conquered in the past with further corrections, differentiations, and insights.[38]

[38] We have exemplified the task of the contemporary philosopher with respect to ethics in a lecture delivered at Catholic University:

"When the ideas of a great philosopher have formed a school and taken on the character of a closed system that can be taught like a textbook, the members of such a school do not even do justice to the master whose disciples they claim to be. Because of the love for a system as such, they are led to overlook several important insights of the master which do not fit into this system.

"[The] rehabilitation of ethics . . . would rather revise traditional ethics by conforming it with reality: the world of moral data offered to us in life, in Holy Scripture, and in the saints. What is required is a rethinking of all the answers in ethics, and this will arise from a close contact with moral reality and with the plenitude of moral values and disvalues.

"Such contact will make it possible to see that in many cases the truths grasped in traditional ethics call for further differentiation, for completion, and for enrichment. Above all, it will make evident the need for a full philosophical grasp of the many realities which are silently presupposed in traditional philosophy, though not explicitly recognized and expressly admitted. In this reflection there will be appreciated the full philosophical meaning of a reality which is known in the immediate, living contact with reality. Such, for example, was Aristotle's appreciation of the four causes. This review also implies the elimination of all the tacit but never proven presuppositions which often bar the way to an adequate knowledge of the real nature of morality. . . ."

But apart from the positive mission of the contemporary Catholic philosopher, there is another one that modern times impose on him. In the morass of present day ideological confusions, it is imperative that the Catholic philosopher unmask widespread philosophical myths, destroy arbitrary constructions, and refute fashionable pseudo-philosophers.

8

The *Kairos*

ST. PAUL EXHORTS TIMOTHY to preach the Gospel *opportune importune*, "in season and out of season."[39]

The Church's mission is independent of circumstances

The mission to preach Christ's message is independent of circumstances. Whether announcement of divinely revealed truth is easy, whether preaching the Gospel provokes persecution of the Church or loses it great advantages are matters that should not influence its apostolate. For example, St. Ambrose would not admit emperor Theodosius to the church in Milan because he permitted the slaying of six thousand innocents in Samos. The grandeur and apostolic courage of this deed are more striking when we recall that Theodosius was the great protector of the Church.[40]

39 2 Tim. 4:2.

40 The attitude of the great Cardinal Saliège, Archbishop of Toulouse, toward the Vichy regime is another outstanding example.

Yet historical circumstances may make particular demands

Yet there exists also a specific call of the historical hour. The thematicity of truth and its promulgation in history play a role in the divine mission of the Church. In a given historical moment something may be more urgently required than formerly. There may be a call for the definition of a new dogma, for an approval or a condemnation, or for any kind of apostolic intervention. There can even be a situation that for many reasons demands that the Church abstain from any condemnation or intervention, although these might be fully justified.

The historical hour may imply an alertness to positive conditions which may present especially favorable opportunities for the Church's pastoral and missionary apostolate. This is what the term *Kairos* specifically refers to.

In order to clarify the meaning of the *Kairos* it will be necessary to analyze briefly the notion of *historical thematicity*. We are not concerned here with historical thematicity in the life of philosophy, with the full philosophical grasping of certain fundamental realities which have previously been tacitly assumed. Rather we shall confine ourselves to historical thematicity as it concerns the mission of the Church.

Particular evils must be condemned

One type of the call of the hour concerns the evil theories that are propagated in a given historical moment by ideological movements or governments.

Such a moment, for example, was the coming to power of National Socialism in Germany. The condemnation of totalitarianism and racism was called for at this very moment. Though these things were evil as such, and would have been evil in any historical period, condemnation of them was made thematic by the fact that National Socialism assumed power in 1933. Before then, the bishops had indeed condemned National Socialism, and membership in the party carried the penalty of excommunication. Unfortunately, however, the German bishops in 1933 failed to uphold this condemnation at the very hour when an even more solemn condemnation was called for.

Now there are two aspects to the thematicity of condemnation. There is first the mission of the Church to speak up as soon as there arises a movement inspired by false and evil theories that are strictly incompatible with the Christian faith. This applies to the condemnation of all heresies. And this, for example, the German bishops did in the case of National Socialism (which began in 1921) before it assumed power.

The second aspect is the unique pastoral and missionary opportunity afforded by a given historical moment. In 1933, for example, there is no doubt that if the bishops had condemned National Socialism with an absolute *non possumus* (veto) and had stood like a rock in the midst of the wavering and intimidated German people, millions could have been converted to the Church. From the missionary point of view it was an hour that comes perhaps once in two hundred years in the life of a country. This is the *Kairos*. It is the special historical opportunity granted to the Church in Her apostolic activity.

There are other types of the call of the hour. These do not have the same impact, nor do they touch the core of the life of the Church in the same way. They relate to what is being called the *aggiornamento*. We are thinking of how the conditions of life in a given epoch in history may give certain opportunities to the apostolic activities of the Church. For example, the enormous technical development of Western civilization today is also part of the call of the *Kairos*.

The conditions of life calling for *aggiornamento*, as well as the prevalent intellectual and moral features of an age, may be neutral, strictly positive, or positive from one point of view and negative from another. But when they are pronouncedly negative and tainted with disvalues — especially with moral disvalues — the call of the hour is for a condemnation.

Because an antipathy to the condemnation of secular "orthodoxies" and religious deviations characterizes the mentality of our time, it is necessary to emphasize that the call of the hour, the opportunity presented to the apostolate of the Church in a particular moment in history, implies not only the exploitation of the positive elements of an epoch, but also the unequivocal condemnation of the errors and evil trends. Condemnation and the unmasking of errors is widely seen today as something hostile to love. No longer understood is the basic principle enunciated by St. Augustine — *interficere errorem, diligere errantem* (kill the error, love the one who errs).[41]

It is assumed that these two actions contradict one another, when in fact love necessarily requires the killing of error. We shall treat this widespread misunderstanding in greater detail in a later chapter. At this point, it may suffice to point out that it is precisely the Church's ultimate love for all human beings that calls for the condemnation of error and that these condemnations are an essential response to the call of the hour.

The condemnations of the great heresies — Arianism, Pelagianism, Nestorianism, and Monophysitism — all issued from a call of the historical moment. The primary theme has certainly always been truth, the protection of divine revelation against all

[41] This sentiment appears with different wording in *The City of God*, Bk. 14, ch. 6.

distortions. But the necessity of condemning a particular heresy at a given moment issues from the call of the time.

A condemnation assumes a heightened thematicity when it deals with the spreading of dangerous error in society or the brutal enforcement of evil errors by a totalitarian state, as in National Socialist Germany or in Communist countries. That this condemnation utters a truth is obviously presupposed; but pastoral responsibility is also highly thematic. To speak the truth at this moment, to protect men against an infectious and ruinous error and to bring through this testimony the light of Christ to many souls outside the Church, is a dramatic feature of the *Kairos*.

Abstention from condemnation is sometimes necessary

Sometimes, however, practical reasons of the highest order may militate against any outright condemnation of an evil. When the moment is *importune*, out of season, in the sense that representatives of the Church itself will be subject to persecution, St. Paul's exhortation clearly applies. No such danger should ever hinder the promulgation of Christian doctrine or any other intervention by the Church.

But when the moment is such that an intervention would only increase the evil against which the Church would protest, the words of St. Paul no longer necessarily apply. Obviously, the circumstances of the hour can impose only an abstention from intervention, never any compromise with error or evil.

This was the case when the Church did not directly and openly attack Hitler in World War II for his terrible persecutions of the Jews. Experience had shown that every intervention of this kind by the Church only resulted in increasing the violence and fury of these persecutions. At this moment the very interest of the persecuted required the Church to refrain from intervention, however valid it would have been as a moral judgment. It is a great oversimplification of the exigencies of history, as well as a disastrous misunderstanding of the call of the *Kairos*, to cry, "The Church has the mission of proclaiming the truth regardless of the consequences!" To speak out on an event and thereby to take advantage of the pastoral opportunity connected with it may increase the evils suffered by the very persons whose sorry plight moved us to action in the first place.

Truth must motivate all responses to the moment

Thus, the *Kairos* presents a very subtle and complex question since many — and sometimes conflicting — factors have to be taken into account. But it is a fateful misunderstanding of the *Kairos* not to make the crucial distinction between the theme of truth and that of history. Given that the historical thematicity makes the promulgation of certain truths especially urgent, the value these promulgations have on account of their truth will be distinct from the value they have on account of the necessity of issuing them at this particular moment. Not only does this latter value presuppose the former (since the promulgation of truth only, and never of error, can be required of the Church by the hour), but the truth of the promulgations always remains the main reason for appreciating them and not their historical thematicity.

Response to the times has its particular dangers

Whenever a man allows historical thematicity to gain the ascendancy over truth, he ceases to be in a healthy relation to truth. He is no longer a real seeker after truth. At the least he is in danger of slipping into the grip of historical relativism. And the power that certain ideas have in an historical moment may induce him to believe that compromise with them will create an opportunity for the victory of Christ. This leads inevitably to missing the true call of the hour, as was the case with the Conference of German Bishops at Fulda in 1933.

In its extreme form this error is widespread among progressive Catholics, who tend to identify the call of the *Kairos* simply with adaptation to the mentality or spiritual climate of an epoch.

The votaries of this adaptation pretend to base their attitude on the words of St. Paul: "I became a Jew to the Jews, that I might win the Jews. . . . I became all things to all men."[42] They interpret his words to mean that the real apostolate implies that we adapt not only ourselves, but also Christ's message, to the peculiar mentality of the persons whom we wish to win for Christ. We must speak their language — and that means taking up their modes of thought and behavior — in order to be able to reach their souls.

Two ways of adapting the Gospel to one's time

Now this can certainly be understood in a fruitful and legitimate sense. But it can also conceal a perversion of St. Paul's meaning. It is necessary therefore to distinguish two different kinds of "adaptation."

It is legitimate to seek the greatest possible knowledge of him to whom we would communicate Christ's word. We should first strive to know his situation, his mentality, his positive and negative tendencies, his yearnings, the truth he has grasped, the errors he has fallen prey to. This is indispensable if we are to know where to begin with our apostolate. We should secondly try with loving reverence to enter through the door already opened by the truths he has grasped, as St. Paul did on the Areopagus when he availed

42 1 Cor. 9:20, 22.

himself of the notion of the "unknown God."[43] Thirdly, we should accept and even endorse all customs that do not contradict the Christian truth and the Christian *ethos*. Fourthly, we should make use of all his more or less conscious yearnings for God.

All the moral values he is familiar with, all the beauty he has discovered in nature, all those natural truths that play a role in his world view and are embedded in his religion would be a starting point for our apostolate. And if there are true and valid elements in his religion (such as a sense of the sacred, a yearning for the absolute, transcendence, genuine piety, genuine recollection), we should make these bridges to the Christian Gospel.

But hand in hand with this, there should go a refusal to make any compromise with the errors in which he is involved, an untiring effort, born out of the love of Christ and charity for this brother, to liberate him from his errors.

It is precisely at this point that St. Paul's words may be forced to yield a false irenicism. Instead of helping to convey the true message of Christ, our effort to adjust to the mentality of the other may so transform that message that acceptance of it no longer requires a conversion. To speak the language of the non-Catholic, therefore, can never mean to falsify the Christian message by translating it into terms incompatible with it, or by offering it according to an *ethos* that contradicts the very atmosphere of Christ.

The attempt to adapt the doctrine of the Church to the mentality of an epoch implies that divine revelation is molded and fashioned according to the spirit of the time. This is a caricature of the call of the *Kairos*. It undermines the very *raison d'être* of the Church and Her apostolate. If the doctrine of the Church is not

[43] Acts 17:23.

based on an immutable divine revelation, but can change with the age, if it is not the same Gospel that is proclaimed at every call of the *Kairos* throughout history, then the very justification of the apostolic mission of the Church (to go and teach all nations[44]) collapses.

[44] Matt. 28:19.

9

Optimism and Christian hope

IT IS COMMONPLACE among many Catholics today to insist that a truly living faith implies an optimistic outlook on the future. Anyone who stresses tradition and warns of what history has taught about human frailty is accused of lacking optimism, courage, and a healthy approach to life. These Catholics believe that such an optimistic ethos is the very test of vitality of faith and openness to the call of the *Kairos*. They accord a crucial importance to the ideas of young people. Their attitude reveals their readiness to accept an opinion on the probability of its being the "voice of the future" rather than because of its truth.

Although it is certainly justified to anticipate future developments, there is no reason whatsoever for favoring an idea chiefly on account of its chances of gaining currency in the future.[45] Here

[45] It is really rather dangerous to believe that one can determine just what elements in the present are indications of the dominant intellectual trends of the future. There have been persons who have had a quasi-prophetic vision of future dangers or trends — persons such as Kierkegaard and Dostoyevsky (especially in *The Devils*) — but in claiming to be able to

again we are confronted with an infringement on rights that truth alone possesses.

These Catholics can see only two possibilities: either we view gloomily the main spiritual currents of our time, which foreshadow a still more threatening future, and withdraw from the world in a mood that combines paralyzing fear with regretful resignation; or we adopt an optimistic outlook on the future — a "healthy attitude" — and consent cheerfully to go along with the times.

But this is another false choice. In fact it misses the really Christian attitude, which combines a sober awareness of all dangers of the situation created by the fall of man with an unshakable hope which results from the faith that Christ has redeemed the world.

Optimism differs from Christian hope

This false choice misses the radical difference between hope and optimism. The confusion of the two constitutes another form of secularization. It is not our task here to enter upon an analysis of the nature of hope. But it should be obvious that in every hope there is a reference to Providence, a trust in a benign intervention of God which upsets the balance fixed by all natural factors. Even if a man claims to have no faith in God, he nonetheless presupposes Providence at the very moment in which he hopes. Hope is altogether different from the attitude of the man who on account of his boundless vitality escapes from despair, even when confronted with the blackest menace. Instead of the humility of hope he exhibits the self-assurance that derives from feeling himself capable of coping with any situation.

discern the spiritual climate of the future we should consider ourselves on very shaky ground.

Christians remain keenly aware of dangers

Our main interest, however, is not the general difference between hope and vital optimism. Rather, we are concerned with the opposition between an optimistic outlook on the development of history and the Christian attitude toward the historical future.

We need only to consider the sober view of the Apostles and the saints in order to see the depth of this opposition. Theirs is by no means an optimistic outlook on the future. They do not think that progress is in any way guaranteed by the immanent development of history. Still less do they manifest the conviction that the Christian should optimistically join the movement of history.

Their attitude shows, instead, an awareness of the continuing struggle between Christ and the spirit of the world and an unshakable hope in God's help in this struggle. They manifest a pitiless detection of all dangers, the actual ones of the present moment and the threatened ones of the future. Simultaneously, however, they manifest an unshakable faith in the victory of Christ. They are neither pessimists nor optimists. They are the only true realists.

Christians entrust the future to God

They see the world as it is, without illusions, but they see beyond the world. Clearly aware of Satan's constant onslaughts on the world, they are firmly grounded in the faith that Christ has redeemed the world. They know that He has called us to fight with Him. They are filled with the consoling and blissful conviction that nothing can separate the man who seeks Christ from His love.

The difference is obvious between this Christian attitude toward the future, which the saints manifested, and the optimistic outlook of the one who approaches the future cheerfully, who sees in history some sort of working of the Holy Spirit.

Christian hope does not blind us to dangers; on the contrary, it rather presupposes that we see reality as it is. But the one who hopes knows that God is above this world. Trusting in Him, in His infinite love, he is protected from depressive resignation. Hope breaks through all immanentism; it is essentially transcendent.

There is certainly rooted in man's vital structure an element of looking forward, of joyful expectation. This is a kind of force propelling us onward; it encourages us to look toward forthcoming activities. This anticipation is certainly a sign of health and a welcome lubricant in the household of man's everyday life. But when it colors our whole attitude toward the future, when it makes us see the future in a rosy light, when it blinds us to the threat of real dangers, and when it becomes mere optimism, it is an illusion-producing narcotic. This is especially evil when the historical future and the mission of the Church are at stake. We may then be fatally prevented from invoking the criterion of truth, from seeing and judging everything in the light of Christ, from following St. Paul's advice to test all things and hold to what is good.[46] We may then succumb to the illusion that by adapting ourselves and the faith to the times, we are responding to the call of the *Kairos*.

A shallow, optimistic, progressive ideology of history will have replaced the holy sobriety and supernatural strength born of hope that we witness in the saints.

[46] 1 Thess. 5:21.

Part II

Dangers of Our Time

10

The Christian attitude toward one's time

WE HAVE EXAMINED at some length the nonsensical demand that Christian revelation be adapted to the spirit of our epoch. In the sixteenth century Cardinal Cajetan summed up the issue when he stated that religion should not be adapted to man; rather, man should be adapted to religion. Yet, if the fallacy in any attempt at adapting Christian revelation to the dominant spirit of an epoch has been set forth in principle, the appalling incompatibility of this effort with the very nature of divinely revealed religion will be fully disclosed when those spiritual and intellectual trends that are typical of our age — and hold such fascination for progressive Catholics — have been scrutinized.

We must have an objective attitude to our own epoch

Far be it from us to reduce the cultural and spiritual complexity of our time to an artificial unity or to overlook the many positive elements that characterize it and then indulge exclusively in praise of the past simply because it is past. But we must be fully alert to the tragic dangers of the time in which we live. As we have insisted, our task is to assume an objective and critical attitude toward our own epoch. Such an attitude has marked many outstanding minds throughout history. There will always be people who drift in the stream of ideas that dominate their time. And there will always be others who are beyond consolation because nothing is the same as it was in their youth, or who are so fascinated by the glow of a departed reality that to them the past seems in everything superior to the present. Both tendencies are unobjective. The former is so because it is overwhelmed by a gregarious instinct. The latter is unobjective because it is hypnotized by a mirage of the past.

But there have also been persons who were neither biased against their own epoch, nor intoxicated by it. These are the really independent personalities, who criticized their time pitilessly in what was objectively evil and recognized what was good and positive.

In the same spirit that animated such men we wish first to indicate the positive features of our epoch and then to delineate the grave dangers that also characterize it.

Many positive elements characterize our modern age

The *aggiornamento* stressed by Vatican II implies that the Church favors all the positive trends of our epoch and assumes them to herself — those that are in their nature compatible with Christ and those that are an outgrowth of the Christian life and spirit. But positive natural features of the time should not be taken into the Christian orbit without their receiving the imprint of Christ. They are, as it were, to be baptized.

One of the purely positive features is the development of *medicine*. This is an obvious benefit to mankind, a progress that is able not only to prevent great personal tragedies in the sea of tears that is human life, but also to prolong the spiritual fecundation of the world by many great minds and personalities.

Another such feature is the *idealism* expressed in the readiness to make great sacrifices in order to help other people, even those of remote countries. This is certainly more developed in today's youth than in the youth of former epochs. We are, of course, abstracting from the sublime devotion of the saints of past centuries and from the heroic work of the missionaries; that is of an altogether different and incomparably higher order. What we have here, rather, is a purely natural kindness, a sensitivity to the sufferings of others and an interest in their earthly happiness, even when they are not known personally.[47]

Some positive elements contain negative dimensions

Other currents of our epoch, however, contain potential dangers. In acknowledging their great value we must not overlook the accompanying dangers, so that we shall be able to separate the positive aspects from the dangers by baptizing the former. We shall thus accomplish the *instaurare omnia in Christo* — the founding of all things in Christ.

Within the orbit of free Europe, Canada, and the United States, the *sense of social justice* is a pervasive aspect of life. In

[47] To be sure, these contemporary deeds can also be motivated by an authentic charity, as was, for example, the work of Dr. Walsh of the hospital ship *SS Hope* and Dr. Dooley in Laos. These actions then assume an incomparably higher value proportionate to their superior motivation. But these cases cannot be considered typical of our epoch. They are, rather, manifestations of Christian charity such as are to be found in all centuries of the Christian era. Of course, the possibility of relieving suffering on a large scale is due to our medical and technological progress and therefore is typical of our epoch.

other times differences in the material conditions of life were too much considered a God-given reality implying no obligation on the fortunate few to improve the situation of those in the lower reaches of society.

Today, however, recognition of the rights of all men to adequate compensation and protection against economic injustice has gained wide currency. This improvement in the conscience of the average man, this widespread awakening of a sense of social responsibility, is certainly a most positive feature of the mentality of our epoch.

But hand in hand with it there goes an *overemphasis on rights*, a *diminishing of gratitude*, and an *overproud antipathy to gifts*. Such attitudes result in a dehumanization of society, in a tendency to replace all personal generosity with institutional legalization, in a dissolution of the joy that only gratitude can bestow when we receive something which we have no right to claim.

This is the evil that tends to accompany a very positive phenomenon of our time. If we are to protect the fruits of social justice from this blight, it is necessary for us to recognize both the good and the evil. We can then separate social justice from the tyranny of trying to force persons by law to assume moral attitudes that by their very nature can only arise spontaneously from the individual's moral conscience.[48]

Another positive feature of our time is the *accessibility of cultural goods* to the generality of people. Culture is no longer thought of as a privilege of "the four hundred." It is, of course, still true that real appreciation of music, literature, and fine arts will always depend on the artistic sense of the individual person,

[48] Obviously, we are not referring here to the many legal forms of protection of the poor, the sick, and the aged which are absolutely positive and imperatively called for.

according to the capacity of the one receiving and, consequently, that there will always be great variation in the understanding of works of art.

But precisely because artistic receptivity is not a function of economic status, the diffusion of culture over an ever wider audience represents a genuine progress. The media for this diffusion are positive as such, and valuable insofar as they serve the transmission of genuine culture — that is, of worthwhile art and good education. But these technological means also facilitate the *diffusion of artistic trash and cheap, even dangerous, ideologies*. They then serve to poison men's minds more thoroughly and universally than was possible hitherto.

Anyone who (quite properly) extols the positive value of these means has the corresponding duty to caution against their abuse and to awaken a sense of responsibility about their employment. For the great concern of the present age to bring culture to people from all walks of life should manifest itself as much in the fight against the diffusion of cultural poison as in the effort to reach ever larger numbers.

As for *technological progress* as such, we must say that it is more than doubtful that the world has really changed for the better because of it. The evils that go hand in hand with the *industrialization and mechanization of the world* are obvious.

But this is one of the few trends in history that are extremely hard to reverse. Whereas it is absolutely false to believe that there is no possibility of changing spiritual things, whereas it is a grave error to believe that some *logos* of history imposes ideologies or mass movements on us (such as Marxism, collectivism, or secularism), there truly are certain trends which cannot be stopped by man's free intervention. Technological progress is one of these trends. We must therefore try to make the best of it. Above all, we must prevent that deformation of our spirit that consists in making of technology a model — a kind of exemplary cause — for all other pursuits. This would be to worship before a computer idol.

Another definitely positive feature of our epoch is the *greater respect to be found for the soul of the child.* The spirit that moved the noble Maria Montessori has grown vastly, and we have witnessed a decline in the practice of beating children and in the general abuse of authority. But this positive feature is also accompanied by an evil tendency. John Dewey's unfortunate ideal, which set up an immanent logic of education that excluded all objective values, has led to the elimination of real education, for it overlooks man's nature as a person — that is, as a being capable of having meaningful intentional relations with the world of objects.

All too many moderns have ignored the great wrong done to a child when all spiritual inspiration and all loving disclosure of values are seen as an infringement on his freedom and when the important functions of true authority and just punishment are deliberately excluded. The new respect for the soul of the child, therefore, should be coupled with a hostility for the accompanying *distorted ideas of education and freedom.*

Christians must respond prudently to the times

It should be clear that we are not by any means blind to the positive aspects of our epoch. But favoring these trends and seizing the opportunities they offer for the apostolate can never consist in mere adaptation. They must be baptized in Christ. And inevitably linked to this process of assumption is the fight against all the negative elements that have been associated with the good features thanks to the deplorable rhythm of reaction and antithesis we discussed above. But here again can be seen the great difference between the decrees of the Council and the ideas and actions of progressive Catholics.

The Christian attitude toward one's time

The progressive Catholics are indiscriminately enamored of the spirit of our age, and they advocate an adaptation of the Church to this spirit. They seldom perceive both the good and evil aspects of the one trend, let alone those that are entirely evil. The attitude called for, however, is the opposite of an indiscriminate one; for one of the great tasks Christians are called upon to perform today is precisely a clear and sober analysis, not only of the good things, but also of the dangers of our time.

11

Historical relativism

IN LOOKING WITHOUT PREJUDICE at many of the intellectual trends of our epoch one cannot but observe a most disastrous phenomenon: the substitution of the socio-historical reality of ideas for their truth.

Certain ideas tend to dominate an age

It is indeed a very interesting fact that in a given historical epoch a great role is played by certain ideas and ideals, by certain intellectual trends, by a certain mentality. We need only recall the role played by the chivalrous attitude of the troubadours, their new approach to women in the twelfth and thirteenth centuries, or the role of rationalism in the eighteenth century, or the romantic mentality at the beginning of the nineteenth century (especially in Germany), and its influence on the approach to life, religion, and philosophy. These and many other available examples force us to acknowledge the existence of an interpersonal, socio-historical reality of ideas, ideals, and attitudes toward life and the universe.

This does not, of course, imply that all the people of any given epoch are dominated by these ideals and attitudes. As we shall see, it would be a great oversimplification to consider a given historical epoch to be a closed entity in which everything is determined (or even merely tainted) by certain common ideals and a common mentality. Anyone who looks at history with unprejudiced eyes and is not caught in the net of Hegelianism cannot but admit that every epoch contains opposed trends, as well as many individual personalities — a Socrates, a St. Augustine, a Pascal, a Kierkegaard — who are independent of the general trend and oppose it in a spirit of great objectivity and intellectual freedom.

But it is nevertheless a fact that in a given epoch certain ideals and intellectual attitudes attain an interpersonal, historical reality to such a degree that we can say that they are "in the air." They are alive; they color and form the spiritual climate of the age. This historical vitality may be restricted to certain countries; or it may be more universal, embracing an entire cultural orbit in a given historical moment.

Truth is not the same as the historical vitality of an idea

Now it is the fatal error of our own time to confuse this interpersonal, social reality, this historical vitality of certain ideologies and attitudes, with their truth, validity, and value. The categories of truth and falsity have been replaced by the question of whether something is active in the present age or belongs to a former epoch, whether it is current or superannuated, alive or dead. Whether something is alive and dynamic seems more important than whether it is true and good. This substitution is a symptom of intellectual and moral decay. Formerly, certain ideas and ideals gained great influence over many minds because of their historical vigor, yet their adherents were nevertheless convinced of their truth and value. But today — apart from their conviction about the truth of an idea — the interpersonal, historical reality of that idea is alone enough to cause people to rave about it and feel sheltered in it.

In this dethronement of truth by the ambiguous notion of vitality the influence of pragmatism is manifest. Questions of truth and value are considered obsolete, abstract, and without interest. The only relevant question seems to be whether an idea is alive, dynamic, operative. This reflects a desire to extend the mode of verification of the hypotheses of natural science (through the observation of their operativeness, their actual *working*) to the ultimate metaphysical realities.

The most striking example of the exclusive interest in such historical-social aliveness (and the concomitant elimination of the question of truth) is the "God is dead" drivel and the extent to which this expression is taken seriously. Obviously, its only possible meaning is that mankind's faith in God is no longer alive. Thus we say that Apollo is dead or Pan is dead. The question of whether God exists in reality patently has no interest for our intellectual morticians, because as soon as this metaphysical question is raised, the answer can only be either that there is a God or there is no God. To say that once God really existed and then He died is completely nonsensical, a contradiction in terms. But truth has been dethroned.

The question of God's objective existence is not so much as raised because it is no longer thought to be important. It is assumed from the beginning that God is a fiction like Apollo, and therefore it is asked only whether or not this obviously fictional idea still has socio-historical vitality. Certainly, one can say that the blue flower of Romanticism is dead, that Greek mythology is dead, and so on. As long as a person asks only whether something is alive in the socio-historical sense, the notion of dying has meaning.

The arguments defending the slogan "God is dead" confirm the dethronement of truth and its replacement by the notion of historical aliveness. One hears such arguments as: "God is dead because he has proved to be inoperative in our age" or "because he no longer fits into our society." The proof of the intellectual and spiritual decay of our time is that these shallow and stupid statements are taken seriously in magazines and in college discussions without the slightest awareness that the question of truth has been silently replaced by the question of mere historical and social reality. Moreover, "God is dead" is considered a new and revolutionary statement, although it is only repeating Nietzsche.

Truth is eternal

This dethronement of truth includes several grave errors. First, there is the error of replacing the never superannuated and noble impact of truth, especially of fundamental metaphysical and religious truth, with the short-lived sociological efficacy and the historical fashionableness of an idea.

The eternal, unchanging nobility and attraction of truth, of which St. Augustine says, "*Quod desiderat anima fortius quam veritatem?*" (What does our soul desire more than truth?), is no longer understood. It has been forgotten that compared with this intrinsic life of truth, the mere sociological reality of an idea is a one-day fly, an ephemeral being destined to be replaced by other ideas, other currents and attitudes, after a longer or shorter passage of time.

Truth should have historical vitality in every epoch

But although it is true that the only reality that false ideas can possess is that of an ephemeral socio-historical aliveness, the acquisition of this social reality may represent the fulfillment of the inner claim of truth. Here, historical aliveness, interpersonal reality, takes on an altogether different character from that found when false ideas are in question. This is especially clear in the case of revealed absolute truth. God exists independently of how many people believe in Him, how many have found Him, and the extent to which faith in God has acquired an historical, interpersonal dominion.

The objective existence of God is infinitely more important than such interpersonal dominion. But the truth of God's existence should acquire this dominion, and in the event that this is accomplished, the social reality assumes a completely new character. We cannot really understand the very phenomenon of socio-historical reality unless we see that true ideas and ideals, and especially the true religion, are meant to acquire interpersonal reality. Then, and only then, does the fact that something is in the air, that it possesses an interpersonal reality, acquire the character of a victory of truth (ultimately, of Christ), rather than that of a merely historical rhythm.

As long as merely cultural factors are at stake, the changing rhythm is rooted in the very nature of history. But here, too, the all important question is whether or not these factors possess an authentic value. The mere fact that certain cultural elements are alive in a given historical era is by no means a reason for praising them — even if that era be our own.

Pluralism of religious "truths" is an evil

Insofar as cultures are concerned, multiplicity has a value, just as does the pluralism of national characters. When, however, it comes to metaphysical or ethical truth — and especially when it comes to religion — any pluralism is an evil.

Evil, too, are the many fluctuations in the life of religion that occur in history. Unlike cultural pluralism, religious pluralism is in no way a sign of life, but rather a symptom of human frailty and insufficiency.

Great metaphysical and ethical truths, and the true religion itself, are destined to take root among men. Here, the "oughtness" of assuming social reality gives to their aliveness a special significance. It represents a descending of Christ into the soul of the individual person and the erecting of His kingdom in the interpersonal sphere. It is the dimension of Christ's victory that He predicted in saying: "Where two or three are gathered together in my name, I am in the midst of them."[49]

To supplant truth in its transcendent existence with a merely social reality is to imprison man and history in a desolate immanentism. On the other hand, the incarnation of transcendent truth in man and history represents the victory of transcendence over the purely immanent.

Historical relativism dethrones truth

The dethronement of truth is the very core of historical relativism. Unlike former types of relativism, it does not deny the possibility of attaining absolute truth; rather, it interprets truth in such a way that conformity with objective existence is replaced by conformity with a mere interpersonal, socio-historical reality.

Thus, Professor Max Muller of Munich claims that the philosopher's real task lies in the conceptual formulation of the trends and ideas which are in the air in the times in which he lives. And it is not uncommon to hear it said that the miracle that was "true" in the Middle Ages is no longer true today, a proposition that would

[49] Matt. 18:19.

be nonsensical if the question of objective truth had not been replaced by that of socio-historical reality.

We also find this substitution — though in another form — in the philosophy of Heidegger. According to him, the statement that the sun revolves around the earth was not wrong before Copernicus discovered that the earth revolves around the sun. In limiting the reality of truth to the act of knowledge he denies all transcendent existence and all transcendent truth.

Historical relativism presupposes truth

The replacement of truth with the socio-historical reality of ideas shares the fate of all relativisms, as well as of all attempts to reinterpret the elementary notion of truth. For some ultimate, basic data can never be denied without re-introducing them tacitly and implicitly. Being, truth, and knowledge are such ultimate data. Much as the historical relativist may claim to be uninterested in the question of truth, caring only for the interpersonal vitality of ideas, he presupposes it in every proposition. In the first place, he is claiming truth for the theory that history is characterized by the ideas "in the air" in various epochs. And the assertion that a particular notion is now "alive" also claims to be true. Obviously, the question can be discussed. The Communist will claim that Marxism is the ideal of the hour, the dynamically growing conviction; the democrat, that it is democracy that fills the air of our epoch. And in this discussion, each claims truth for his thesis — truth in the classical, inalterable, basic meaning of the term.

It is usually assumed by those concerned that the shift of interest from truth to the socio-historical reality of an idea is legitimate and constitutes a progress. Here, again, the truth of this assumption is tacitly maintained — namely, that the shift is truly a progress, truly the right thing to do.

The same applies to the notion that the task of the philosopher is to formulate the ideas "in the air." When it comes to their own statements, Max Muller and Martin Heidegger arrogate truth in its original sense. There can be no doubt that a man who contrives the most absurd interpretation of truth cannot but presuppose the authentic notion of truth and thereby offer the best and most eloquent refutation of his "new" interpretation.

Popular ideas have the appearance of objectivity

The historical vitality of ideas obviously plays an enormous role in making many naive people accept something as true. For uncritical minds the fact that certain ideas have many adherents is a powerful argument for their truth. That these ideas come to them totally from without gives them an appearance of objectivity, of a validity independent of their own preferences, and they therefore accept them as true. For many others it may be social pressure operating on their gregarious instinct that makes them swallow these ideas. These are the classical ways *doxa* (opinion) originates.

Historical relativism lacks interest in the question of truth

This susceptibility to the dynamism of popular ideas has always existed as a typical frailty of the human mind. This is very different from the modern lack of interest in truth and intoxication with the vitality of ideas. In the former case, the interpersonal, historical reality of an idea is taken as proof of its validity or forces the unwitting acceptance of it; at any rate, the idea is considered to be true, and not merely "in the air." In the case of modern historical relativism, on the contrary, truth is explicitly replaced by a sociological reality. The question to be asked of an idea or theory becomes, "Is it alive? Does it fit the mentality of our present age?"

12

Evolutionalism, progressivism, and progress

TWO OTHER dangerous contemporary trends are evolutionalism and progressivism. These ideologies differ from historical relativism in that they do not replace truth by the socio-historical reality. They consider each succeeding epoch to be superior in value and nearer to truth. They are thus not relativist in the same way. However, they both share with historical relativism the unfortunate illusion of the superiority of the present age over former times.

Evolutionism sees mankind's spiritual progress as automatic

Evolution and progress are not identical notions. Evolution refers to the ontological sphere. It is the scientifically unproven theory that higher beings have resulted from lower ones, or that lower beings have been transformed into higher ones. Whether such an evolution exists in the realm of impersonal nature is very much contested. But to extend the concept of evolution to historical man, to the history of mankind, obviously makes no sense.

There are no symptoms of ontological change in the bodily structure of historical man sufficient to indicate either a movement forward or the acquisition of new spiritual capacities, such as intellect or free will. And this is the only way in which the notion of evolution could properly apply to historical man. At this point evolution ceases to be a scientific hypothesis and becomes a most unscientific ideology: *evolutionalism*.

The idea of a movement onward and upward, a movement that displays itself independently of man's free will, of his conscious, intentional acts — in a word, of his free collaboration — is meaningless when applied to man's spiritual life (to his knowledge of, and his responses to, the world endowed with values, as manifested in friendship, love, and morality).

Those who want to extend the notion of evolution to the history of mankind are in fact uninterested in man as a person. They replace morality with an immanent process of improvement leaving no room for man's free decisions. This is a radical depersonalization and it is one of the many grave errors in the "theology fiction" of Teilhard de Chardin.

Progressivism holds that human culture always improves

Progress refers to a qualitative movement rather than an ontological movement. The distinction between evolutionalism and progressivism, however, is blurred, because while progress refers to the history of mankind only, and implies man's collaboration, in progressivism progress assumes an automatic character.

But the thesis of progressivism is by no means confirmed by the facts of human history. Indeed, it is flatly contradicted by it. Progress can be spoken of in certain domains only.

It is true that in the course of history man has acquired an incomparably greater knowledge of the material world. In the natural sciences, in medicine, and especially in technology in the widest sense of the term, an enormous progress has been achieved.

When it comes to the question of a truly human life, when we look at history from the point of view of true humanism, it is impossible to conclude that real progress has been achieved. There are ascents in cultural achievement followed by descents. There are epochs of extraordinary cultural and spiritual plenitude, dominated by an overwhelming multiplicity of geniuses. But periods such as fifth-century Athens or fourteenth and fifteenth-century Florence are mysterious gifts which are anything but the result of a steady progress. An automatic progress in human history which would, like growth, imply that every step forward in time necessarily leads to a higher level of existence is obviously out of the question. Who could claim that the second century before Christ was on a higher cultural level than was the fifth century before Christ in Athens? It is impossible to overlook the obvious ups and downs that take place in history with respect to culture and true humanism. But if the claim that there is a steady movement upward is totally unwarranted, the same may be said for the thesis of a progress characterized by two steps forward and one step backward. The facts do not support even such irregular progress.

Dehumanization has accompanied recent material progress

The vast progress that will continue to be made in the natural sciences, in the exploitation of nature, in technology and medicine, in no way entitles us to speak of a general progress of mankind in history. For every man with a sense of culture, the enormous decline that has taken place today in art, architecture, and music is obvious. And no one can deny a general decline in the field of philosophy. If we compare the philosophy of Plato and Aristotle, of St. Augustine and St. Thomas, of Descartes, with logical positivism, pragmatism, and behaviorism, which have had such an influence on modern life, it is impossible honestly to speak of a progress. The same applies to the rhythm of life, to customs, above all, to standards of morality. Nor has there been a progress in reverence, in depth — that is, in true humanism.

Indeed, one can observe signs of a progressive dehumanization. This is camouflaged by the massive material progress. But there is no doubt that hand in hand with the triumph of technology there has gone a dehumanization in the quality of life. Gabriel Marcel has unmasked this process in his book *Man Against Mass Society* and C. S. Lewis has discussed it in his *Abolition of Man.* We shall return to the problem of dehumanization in later chapters.

These trends may suddenly disappear; a reaction, not to say a revenge of human nature, may take place. But then, this would only show that we can speak of human history as a whole neither as a movement downward nor a movement upward. A progress in the full human sense may occur in the life of the individual person or in certain sectors of human activity, but not in man's general moral achievement and approach to life.

Political freedom is not greater everywhere today

To those who would object that there is at least a progress in history in the direction of greater political freedom and greater respect for man's dignity and individual rights, two replies can be made. First, the political face of our century is marked not only by the democracies of America and Europe, but also by Communist rule over a great part of humanity, which certainly represents the most systematic and deliberate denial of the dignity and rights of man that has ever been seen. It surpasses all former savage autocracies. Ours is also the century that spawned National Socialism, another, though less extensive, totalitarian system.

A purely psychological approach degrades man

Second, individual political rights are only one aspect of respect for human dignity. Many of the features of the democratic countries of our era amount to an enormous regression in achieved human dignity. Human engineering is not confined to Communist countries. And the disastrous amoralism widespread in so many societies of the modern world is a much more profound perversion of human dignity than any political slavery.

The increasing blindness to true human dignity expresses itself, for example, in the way even the most horrible sexual perversions (such as sodomy) are shown in movies and even recommended by some psychiatrists. Such aberrations have always existed, but their abominable anti-moral, anti-human character was clearly recognized. The growing acceptance of them is a last notch of dehumanization and depersonalization and, at least in the Christian era, was never to be found before. The attempt to substitute a psychological (or sociological) approach to man and his activity for a moral one amounts to a failure to take man seriously as a person; it is a denial of his dignity, of his transcendence, and his freedom.

The greatest mark of human dignity is man's capacity to be a bearer of moral values, to be responsible for his actions. Man is a metaphysical being by his very nature, and this metaphysical, transcendent character is indissolubly linked to his moral freedom. If we draw man out of the orbit of moral good and evil, we are doomed to ignorance of his authentic nature; we deal with an "it," no longer with a personal being. It is quite ironic that this pseudo-psychological approach is commonly considered a kinder attitude toward persons, an indication of greater empathy or sympathy for them, than the moral approach. In reality it is the greatest offense to human dignity.

Cultural riches are cumulative through time

It might be maintained that there is obviously progress in history in that the human universe grows richer with each contribution, regardless of the general cultural level of a given period or sequence of periods. And it is indeed true that if we abstract from the general achievement of an historical period and only consider the accumulation of the spiritual and cultural riches of former periods which tradition renders potentially accessible to the living, then the human universe is always becoming objectively richer. But this enrichment cannot properly be called a progress.

It is true that a man living in the nineteenth century could profit from the fact that the world had been enriched by the architectural marvels of the Middle Ages as well as by the spiritual glory of Greek antiquity, by the great world of music of the seventeenth, eighteenth, and nineteenth centuries and by the unique blossoming of painting and sculpture of the Renaissance.

What Bernard of Chartres said of philosophy — that we now see more because we are standing on the shoulders of past spiritual giants, such as Plato, Aristotle, and St. Augustine[50] — is true for the entire spiritual world. Men became incomparably richer in the time in which the spiritual treasures of Dante, Shakespeare, Cervantes, Molière, Goethe, and Dostoyevsky were added to those of Aeschylus and Sophocles. How much more meaningful has the human universe become through Bach, Mozart, and Beethoven.

Mankind's access to cultural riches is not cumulative

But though such an enrichment has taken place in the course of time, there has also been an analogous impoverishment. How

[50] As quoted in John of Salisbury, *Metalogicon*, Bk. 3, Ch. 4.

many glorious works of art have been destroyed by war, by fire, by inundations and other forces of nature? How much of nature has been ruined by industrialization? How many marvelous buildings have been destroyed to be replaced by factories and other purely functionalist disfigurements? Further, there is no guarantee that the people to whom tradition offers a greater wealth of cultural treasure will be able to appreciate this gift. Their intellectual and spiritual level may have declined to such an extent that they do not understand their superior cultural inheritance.

Thus, the objective enrichment does not mean a progress for succeeding periods of history. On the contrary, they can sink to a much lower level than previous epochs for all the accumulated stock of spiritual achievements bequeathed them. All the more can it be said that the growth of the human universe in history, through all the cultural treasures, all the great insights and inventions, scarcely implies that the contribution or spiritual level of a later period will be greater than that of an earlier one.

If anything, later generations find it rather more difficult than former ones to create great works. The achievements of the Greeks in sculpture have at times been matched, but never surpassed. The same is true of Dante, Shakespeare, Cervantes, and Michelangelo; later epochs have thrown up no peer. Creative art is a mysterious individual gift.

Philosophical development is not cumulative

Bernard of Chartres was right that, with regard to philosophy, it is indeed possible for us to see more than the giants of the past, thanks to them. Even if we made use of this great advantage, however, to delve a pace further into the truth, our contribution would not in all likelihood be greater than that of the giants on whose shoulders we stand. This is precisely what the famous remark was meant in humility to convey. The magnitude of Plato's contribution to philosophy has never been surpassed; but another giant standing on his shoulders, St. Augustine, conquered a new realm of truth. Unfortunately, the history of philosophy shows that in general this standing on the shoulders does not take place. On the contrary, we often find the valid truths conquered in the past ignored and even denied. Only in the natural sciences is there an immanent logic leading to both a judicious use of the fruits of past speculation and further contributions — that is, a progress.

Progressivism and evolutionalism are evil illusions. They both engender an unwarranted and indiscriminate enthusiasm for all that is new and an optimism that blinds to the dangers of the present epoch.

Progressivism hinders progress

The disciples of progressivism are the very gravediggers of any potential progress. In revolting against tradition, in believing themselves superior to their ancestors, in expecting automatic progress, they forego the very advantage of which Bernard of Chartres speaks. They refuse to stand on the shoulders of giants; rather, they vainly stand on their own feet in the illusion that they can see more than the giants because the automatic progress of history has made them giants.

Evolutionism depersonalizes man

In evolutionalism, as propagated, for example, by Teilhard de Chardin, the disastrous consequences are clearer still. The application to historical man of a purely biological theory implies in reality a complete amoralism, for the perfecting process excludes free will.

The inevitable depersonalization implicit in Teilhard de Chardin's vague theories is most manifest in his ideal of "superhumanity," a final stage in which the individual person is absorbed into a common consciousness.

Personal spiritual progress is possible

Since we have shown that the notion of an automatic progress in history is not in the slightest confirmed by the facts and hence is illusory, it may be proper to suggest the nature of true progress.

In the first place, there can be a progress in the life of the individual person. This has nothing to do with a change in our convictions; it refers rather to an improvement in our living up to true moral ideals. Real progress in one's spiritual life thus implies continuity and fidelity to unchangeable values. By no means can it be considered an evolution. But the stability of our commitment to certain truths and values is accompanied by an increasing practical conformity to them.

We shall deal with religious progress in greater detail in Part IV. For the moment we wish only to stress that continuity and perseverance are the warp and woof of progress in the Christian life. Progress in the direction of an ever more faithful imitation of Christ, of letting ourselves be more and more transformed by Christ, clearly implies both fidelity to Him and unshakable faith in Him. Every turning to false prophets is not only a regression that destroys whatever progress has been achieved, but is also an outright apostasy.

Authentic progress, therefore, refers to a change in the extent to which one lives up to the true goal of one's life. Our goal does not change, but we grow in the fulfillment of our moral obligations, in the acquisition of moral virtues, in conscientiousness, faithfulness, and perseverance. This is the progress for which everyone should aim and hope and *which can be attained with the grace of God*.

There can also be an authentic progress on the level of society. It consists in a greater conformity between social life and the immutable God-willed norms.

Conversion is far more than progress

But when a person undergoes a complete moral change, when he abandons morally wrong ideas or overcomes moral blindness and finds his way to true morality, it would be an extreme understatement, not to say grossly misleading, to speak of a *progress*. In this case one is confronted with a conversion, a *metanoia*, a transition from error to truth, from evil to good, a radical change in conviction and in personal spiritual goals. To call this *progress* is to falsify the event. It is not an ascension from a lower to a higher level, but a passage from darkness to light, a turning from evil to good.

It belongs to the very nature of man as a being placed under the obligation of immutable norms to strive for progress in his own life and in the lives of others and to strive for progress in justice and peace in society. This progress has nothing to do with the automatic progress of evolutionalism and progressivism. And of course it is completely antithetical to historical relativism or the shifting historical vitality of ideas.

True progress depends on moral responsibility

We repeat: progressives are the gravediggers of real progress. Their assumption that automatic progress is the law of history denies the moral responsibility on which true progress depends. If they were right we would not have to strive for progress. Their desire to replace all received truths and values with the latest ideas undermines fidelity and perseverance through which true progress is achieved. For them it is the course of history that informs us about the validity and value of a goal, and not the nature of this goal. Their idolatry of progress, therefore, is no more than intoxication with the illusion of their own superiority. The progressives replace continuity with discontinuity and make progress, which consists precisely in advancing toward an unchanging goal, impossible. In their confusion of change as such with vitality they have forgotten Plato's dictum: "Any change whatever except from evil is the most dangerous of all things."[51]

[51] *Laws*, No. 797.

13

Science fetishism

IN OUR TIME the natural sciences and their methods have increasingly become a pattern for all knowledge. Even such attributes as *objective*, *critical*, *serious*, *reliable*, and *sober* are more or less identified with *scientific*, and the notion of the scientific is thought of more or less exclusively in terms of the natural sciences.

The result has been that the systematic study of any topic has been more and more dominated by the attempt to achieve the kind of objectification and neutralization that takes place in laboratories.

Such is the strong magical appeal of the model of the natural sciences for sophisticated intellectuals of our age that when dealing with subjects utterly different from those of natural science — as in anthropology, sociology, and psychology — their greatest satisfaction is to declare that their analysis is "scientific."

By this they wish to communicate that their approach has been analogous to that of the natural sciences and, above all, that it bears no relation to philosophy. They ignore the fact that different subjects require different methods of inquiry, and pass over the fact that their violent appropriation of the methods of natural science in reality implies a philosophical position.

But the approach that is so fertile in the natural sciences is a deadly poison in the humanities and leads inevitably to superficiality, to the obscuration of the real, and to pseudo-science.

True science and philosophy are not in conflict

Real science in no way crowds out philosophy. An unprejudiced scientist knows that philosophy and science have very different subjects and aims and that their methods of exploration must differ accordingly. It is generally conceded today that scientific questions cannot be answered by philosophy. Unfortunately, it is not so well understood that philosophical questions can never be answered by science. This applies to many professors of philosophy as well as to the generality of the half-educated intellectuals of our time. To the extent that these men consider philosophical questions at all serious and worthy of analysis, they assume that the methods of inquiry and verification of natural science can alone provide the answers.

Mixing science into philosophy threatens transcendence

The invasion of the sphere of philosophy by science in our epoch means that we are being engulfed by immanentism. Despite the arrogant boasts of those who would extend the objectification of the laboratory to all human questions, this immanentism results in the destruction of the capacity for philosophical knowledge. It reverses the process whereby man emerges from the network of actuality and through this distancing is able to wonder at and question what Gabriel Marcel calls the mysteries of being. This emancipation began with the Pre-Socratics in early Greece and culminated in Plato and Aristotle. It was essentially a process of freeing man from a purely pragmatic approach, of transforming *homo faber* (man the maker) into *homo sapiens* (man the knower).

This development resulted in the golden age of Greek philosophy. It was responsible for analogous intellectual triumphs in many other domains. It also gave birth to science. The crowding out of philosophy, the mother of sciences, in the name of science that is commonly attempted today is a retrogressive process in which the glorious emancipation of the spirit is given up. All the sophisticated laboratory techniques and talk of objectivity mask a sinking back into things, a lapse into immanentism. Philosophical inquiry, with its liberation from the fetters of pragmatism, is in reality being replaced by a laboratory objectification loaded with pragmatism. This amounts to a bartering of philosophical consciousness and sensitivity and depth of intuition, which come with the desire for transcendence, for the blank factuality of pure immanentism.

True realism acknowledges man's transcendence

The gravediggers of philosophy deceive themselves into believing that they are the authentic realists, as opposed to the abstract and unrealistic philosophers. But true realism implies above all an awareness of man's metaphysical situation and a wondering inquiry into the ultimate realities that form the basis of the spiritual universe and of man's life. True realism consists precisely in keeping oneself from being overwhelmed by the merely pragmatic necessities of life. It sees beyond that level of reality about which natural science can inform us and turns neither to a lofty world of fiction nor to abstract hypotheses, but to the ultimate, unchanging realities which are inescapably presupposed by rational inquiry (truth, knowledge, and the laws of logic) and by human life (moral good and evil, free will, responsibility, happiness, and love) and which are every man's crucial concern from the moment he awakens to his metaphysical situation.

Correlative to this fetishization of science is the epistemological prejudice that our knowledge of a being has greater certitude the lower it ranks metaphysically. A physiological process in our brain thus seems to be a much more serious and indubitable reality than an inference. This is looking at the universe *à la baisse* (focusing on its lowest aspects). It takes it for granted that an instinct is more real than a meaningful response such as joy, though the latter is certainly not less given in its full reality. This attitude leads to the reduction of spiritual reality to the level of low-ranking data through the nonsensical *nothing-but* method. Thus, love, for example, is taken to be nothing but sex.

The laboratory approach distorts many realities

Perhaps the most dangerous effect of science fetishism is that every aspect of human life is being made an object of laboratory analysis — a process that puts living contact with reality in jeopardy. Sexual intercourse, the most intimate, mysterious union in marriage, categorically precludes laboratory observation. Something that of its very nature is supposed to be a mutual self-donation, a loving interpenetration of souls, can never at the very moment of its accomplishment serve as material for a scientific experiment. A married couple who consent to be observed and photographed in this act not only degrade this mystery of union, but corrode its very nature through the improper approach to it. Any attempt at observation will so modify the entire psychological aspect that the true nature of the events will be falsified and only fake scientific results attained.

There are many other things that by their very nature preclude such an analysis. If, for example, a person tried to evoke contrition in order to give a psychologist an opportunity to study this "phenomenon," or if he attempted to pray so that his expression could be recorded for "science," neither the contrition nor the prayer could be authentic.

The laboratory approach improverishes human experience

The dehumanizing influence that this kind of experimentation has on the approach to life of its victims is much more significant than the falsification of science it entails. Objectification and reductive neutralization depersonalize people's lives. The fact that books like that of Masters and Johnson (who purport to subject sexual intercourse to scientific investigation) are on the best-seller lists is indicative of the moral devastation wrought by science fetishism. These authors present to the reader a fake reality which perverts the psyche of whoever accepts it as real. A similar danger is embodied in the false self-observation and self-consciousness fostered by many psychoanalysts. The intimacy, privacy, and thematicity of such experiences, their intrinsic validity, are doomed by such reductive science. This impoverishment of human experience is destructive of a healthy approach to life, as well as of any true happiness, and it will lead to an unprecedented moral decay. This latter has disastrous consequences, for it affects men's relation to God, their salvation.

Many values are greater than those related to science

Behind all of these dehumanizing practices is the idolization of science, an attitude that results in the attempt to reduce all things to the level at which they will be fit objects for study according to the canons of natural science. The massive material success of science has made it seem to many a panacea. It suffices to claim that a thing must be attempted *for the sake of science* in order to silence all objections. Nonetheless, although the achievements of science are in themselves great and great are its benefits to mankind, it is absurd to believe that science is man's highest good, let alone the highest good in itself.

One need only consider the words of Socrates — "It is better for a man to suffer injustice than to commit it"[52] — in order to realize the inherent superiority of moral values to science, as well as the higher objective good they represent for man. Also, it is extremely doubtful that science has a higher value than genuine art, that a scientific discovery is in itself superior to, say, Shakespeare's *King Lear*, Beethoven's Ninth Symphony, or Michelangelo's Medici Tombs. Is not the good which these represent for humanity, the happiness which they bestow on man, the enrichment they offer the human universe, greater than the benefits science gives us? This is, of course, subject to discussion; but it seems to me that the superiority of great works of art is obvious.

In any case, the superiority of moral values cannot for a moment be contested. Did not Christ say: "What does it profit a man if he gain the whole world, but suffer the loss of his own soul?"[53] And equally superior to science is the integrity of a truly human life. Love, marriage, children — these are more significant goods than natural science and scientific exploration. The possession of metaphysical and moral truth, the knowledge of the true meaning of life, of the destiny of men, and the facts with which this truth is concerned have an incomparably greater impact and existential import for man than science.

Nonetheless, all of these areas of human concern are reduced or ignored by the fetishization of science.

[52] Plato, *Gorgias* 469C, 527B.

[53] Matt. 16:26.

Moral good and evil are the axis of the spiritual universe

False philosophies masked as social sciences interpret moral good and evil as mere taboos. Books and articles help to spread this amoralism by speaking of promiscuity and other moral perversions in a neutral tone. The science fetishists believe that life will be happier and freer if moral good and evil are eliminated in favor of a laboratory approach to all human affairs.

They fail to see that the categories of moral good and evil are at once the axis and the atmosphere of the spiritual universe. Without them, human life loses all grandeur and depth, all color and tension; without them, life becomes an endless boredom. The elimination of moral good and evil in favor of a neutral, "scientific" outlook is the cancer of our epoch. It devours the very basis of a fully human life: the spiritual articulation that was present through all the centuries of the Christian era.

Furthermore, it is a break with the entire spiritual tradition of mankind. And this disintegration — which has been called a movement back to Neanderthal man — is accompanied by the most unwarranted pride. All former epochs are looked down on. The present age is supposed to be superior in intelligence and courage, in spiritual honesty, in liberation from taboos and the fetters of convention. But when we consider these claims of intelligence, honesty, and liberation against the background of the actual moral disintegration of life, they can only be regarded as symptoms of lack of intelligence, a dishonesty, and an imprisonment in pride and concupiscence.

14

Freedom and arbitrariness

A PERVERSE CONCEPTION of freedom prevails today that experiences the universality and objectivity of truth, and the fact that it is withdrawn from our arbitrariness, as a demeaning infringement on our freedom. The inherent exclusivity of truth, the elimination of other possibilities (especially in metaphysical and ethical truth) is seen as an unwelcome obligation to a commitment.

We might compare this condition to that of soldiers who inhaled poison gas in World War I and then experienced fresh air (which to the healthy man is invigorating and wholesome) as unbearably stifling. In like manner, those modern men who have become intoxicated with their own arbitrariness are no longer able to experience the liberating power of truth.

Truth sets us free

Such men do not recognize in the stability and univocality of absolute truth something that liberates us from the fetters of immanentism and self-centeredness and that grants us the awful privilege of transcendence. Christ said: "The Truth shall make you free."[54] This applies primarily to divine, revealed truth, yet every fundamental metaphysical and ethical truth has an analogously liberating effect. For there is a profound relationship between genuine personal freedom and the obligatory commitment that truth imposes.

The grandeur of man's free will consists precisely in the possibility of conforming to the call of objective values, despite the contrary pull of instincts, moods, or other distractions. Man's essential transcendence consists in the twofold conformation of mind and will to objective reality, in his knowledge of truth, and in his free obedience to the call of morally relevant values — ultimately, to the call of God.

Man's dignity comes from his free will

Moreover, the sublime value of being free from external coercion is revealed only when seen against the background of the true nature of man's interior freedom. Why is it so serious to violate the dignity of a person through coercion of any kind? Why are we rightly outraged when we learn that institutions or governments are attempting to prevent a man from acting as his conscience dictates?

There can only be one answer: man's dignity consists in his being endowed with the power of self-determination. This freedom of will is the very opposite of anarchic arbitrariness. It means that man has the power of overcoming the great enemy of his freedom: his own self-centeredness, his own pride and concupiscence. Any coercion implicitly ignores this. Coercion jeopardizes man's transcendence in that it prevents his exercising his ability

[54] John 8:32.

freely to conform to what he clearly recognizes as good, to what he is called upon to accept and do.

Now, if we consider man to be an animal devoid of free will or if we interpret his freedom as mere arbitrariness which leaves him therefore cut off from the meaning and value of being and from God, external coercion ceases to be wrong. Coercion exerted on dogs and horses is not wrong. Cruelty and brutality to animals are of course reprehensible and indeed evil, but coercion of animals does not necessarily involve cruelty.

Fulfillment of obligations perfects freedom

Those who insist that obligations are incompatible with our freedom are actually implying the impossibility of man's ever forming any society and accepting its obligations. For the existence of human society presupposes each man's capacity for transcending himself in freely accepted obligations. Far from being incompatible with true freedom, obedience to moral obligations constitutes the perfection of man's transcendent freedom.

Truth liberates man from repressions

But truth also defines freedom. Those whom illusion cuts off from reality are deprived of the freedom that only truth can guarantee. The hope of extricating man from the tyranny of repressions presupposes an intimate relation between freedom and truth. When certain things are drawn from the unconscious into the clarity of consciousness, it is expected that a liberation will follow this confrontation with reality. Of course, the liberation will be of very doubtful worth as long as the person only becomes conscious of a repression and does not judge it in the light of metaphysical and ethical truth. It is typical of some psychoanalysts that they fail to distinguish between real guilt and a guilt complex. They ignore the overwhelming reality of the categories of moral good and evil. Their illusory world view blunts the conscience of man and deprives him of true freedom, however cheerful he may feel after the "operation."

The essential relationship between freedom and truth is clearly set forth in the unique process of liberation that takes place in authentic and deep contrition. For in contrition man emerges from the fog of the self-illusions generated by pride and enters into the bright, liberating light of truth.

Education should inculcate right values

Resistance to truth in the name of freedom is seen in the modern condemnation of the most legitimate form of influence, which is the exposure of the young to genuine values. Education should offer to the young the religious, metaphysical, and ethical truths the possession of which will protect them from illusion because they lie at the core of reality. A proper education should present these truths in an atmosphere that will facilitate the discovery of their value. But it is just this essence of education that many consider an infringement on the freedom of youth. In reality, they are cutting off the minds of the young from the most important reality and thereby actually inculcating a habit of ignorance of, if not a willful hostility to, the most important truths.

Democracy depends on freedom, not arbitrariness

The doctrine of freedom that sees a threat in the idea of absolute truth undermines what many in this country consider the only absolute value — namely, democracy. Democracy as a mode of political and social existence implies the acceptance not only of objective values that are beyond all discussion, but also of inalterable obligations. True democracy stands or falls with the clear distinction between freedom and arbitrariness.

The reason for the incompatibility of freedom and all types of human engineering and thought control should now be clear. Many moderns flatter themselves with the confidence that they live in an age in which the freedom of the person is fully respected. They overlook the human engineering and milder forms of brainwashing that exist in democratic countries and which constitute a serious disrespect for the dignity and freedom of the person. This kind of disrespect existed much less in former times.

15

Sham honesty

FATHER HANS KÜNG claimed in a speech given at the Council (and he has since repeated the theme on many occasions) that we live in an age characterized by intellectual and moral honesty. It seems to us that Fr. Küng is possessed by an illusion that is especially widespread today.

Some claim that our age is characterized by honesty

There are many who would agree that our present approach to life is much more honest, more "authentic," than that of the Victorian era with all its hypocrisy, conventionalism, and prudery. No longer does public opinion condemn things which most people have always done clandestinely anyway. No longer do we feel obliged to exhibit a polite and friendly demeanor when we actually feel nothing resembling friendliness. No longer are rigid, artificial, empty forms superimposed on our lives. No longer do we feel obliged to cling to traditional opinions. Modern man speaks his own personal opinions in full sincerity. Even if a received idea or teaching is beautiful and uplifting to the spirit, he still wishes to be realistic about it, to guard against comforting illusions. He wants to see reality as it is. The ascendancy of science in our time testifies to the intellectual honesty of our epoch.

But if we analyze this case for the special honesty of contemporary man we shall discover that it is in reality only a sham honesty.

Sinfulness is not necessarily dishonesty

In the first place, it is quite mistaken to believe that a person who does not live up to his moral ideals is therefore dishonest, or, to put it otherwise, that consistent agreement between one's principles and one's conduct is the criterion of honesty. It is certainly desirable for a man to live up to his moral convictions, provided that they are valid. But the all too frequent discrepancy between conduct and conviction is a tragedy rooted in man's fallen nature. This is the perennial conflict of which Ovid says: "*Video meliora proboque; deteriora sequor* (I see and approve what is better; I pursue what is worse)."[55] And St. Paul puts it: "For the good that I will, I do not; but the evil that I will not, that I do."[56] This by no means implies a dishonest character.

To be sure, if a man does not intend to do what he recognizes to be morally right, if he can be indifferent to the moral necessity of action following upon principle, if he does what he knows to be morally wrong without suffering a burdened conscience, then morally, he is a very poor person indeed. But to say that he is dishonest is a great understatement. He is far worse than dishonest. His conduct betrays either a cynical wickedness or a brutish moral unscrupulousness.

[55] Ovid, *Metamorphoses*, Bk. 7.

[56] Rom. 7:19.

However, the man who strives and fails to live up to what he has recognized to be morally good cannot in the least be said to be dishonest. On the contrary, for him to admit that the moral law and moral values are fully valid (even though he has failed to live up to them) is a definite indication of his honesty.

"Adapting" truth to fit our actions is dishonest

What is dishonest — and what is unfortunately typical of our age — is for men to adapt truth to suit their actions: to take their own actual conduct as the standard and to deny the validity of moral laws because they have not succeeded in living up to those laws.

Thus, before we can conclude anything from the formal agreement between a man's moral convictions and his life, we have first to inquire whether this agreement is the result of his living up to his convictions or of his adjusting his convictions to fit his actions. If the former is the case, we must also ask if his moral convictions are true or false, good or evil.

Men who hold shallow, relativistic theories of morality, who may even consider moral precepts to be mere taboos, nevertheless often manage in concrete situations to give the morally right responses (for example, to shrink from committing an act of cruelty or injustice) because in their immediate contact with reality they are, in fact, aware of the ultimate validity and power of moral values.

Men are in general more intelligent and closer to truth in their existential contact with life than in their theoretical reasonings about it. In such cases, agreement between action and theoretical conviction is nothing to be approved; rather, inconsistency between conviction and action is desirable and the question of honesty does not arise.

Shamelessness is not a form of honesty

It is another grave error to believe that a man who has become morally blind and therefore openly acts immorally is more honest than one who seeks to conceal his immorality. It is surely deplorable for men to hide their immoral deeds only out of fear of public opinion. But the man who sees nothing wrong, for example, with promiscuity and speaks of it shamelessly is certainly no better. Nor is he honest or sincere. For the so-called Victorian hypocrite at least betrayed by his hypocrisy an indirect respect for moral values. On the other hand, the shameless contemporary sinner, who has lost all sense of the immorality and meanness of sexual promiscuity, deserves not the slightest praise for his "honesty," for he has no reason to hide his moral deviations. He no longer considers them shocking and he has nothing to fear from public opinion since it has now become fashionable not to be shocked by promiscuity. What once entitled the Bohemian to regard himself as a revolutionary — the fact that he brazenly flouted public opinion — no longer obtains. It is therefore difficult to understand why shamelessness should today be praised as courageous and honest.

Giving scandal should be avoided

Furthermore, there is a perfectly good reason for hiding our sins from the view of society. We are obliged to avoid giving a bad example or scandal to others. This bears no resemblance to the case of Tartuffe, the rascal who sanctimoniously assumes the role of a truly virtuous person with the intention of cheating others attracted by his apparent virtue. This is an extreme of dishonesty. The antithetical honesty here is not to be found in the shameless sinner who feels no need to cloak his sinfulness, but in the virtuous man who hides his virtues out of humility.

Behavior does not always have to mirror feelings

Another false conception of honesty widespread today appears in the assertion that our outward behavior should be in full agreement with our inner feelings and moods. A man who employs expressions of politeness that do not correspond with his true feelings is thus considered dishonest. No doubt, we can rightly speak of a certain dishonesty or lack of genuineness when a man behaves as if he were deeply moved, or overjoyed, or indignant, while actually experiencing nothing of the kind.

It is nevertheless completely wrong to make our actual feelings the sole determinant of our outward behavior toward other persons. Rather, our behavior should conform to what our attitude *should* be. Whatever our real feelings about others, we should be polite and attentive to them. This is by no means dishonest — any more than it is an indication of honesty to be unfriendly, impolite, and inattentive to another person because we do not care for him.

This false conception of honesty idealizes self-indulgence and letting oneself go. It precludes (indeed, repudiates) the enrichment of life that observance of proper forms makes possible. It ignores the moral significance and educational function of such forms of social intercourse. That which constitutes the superiority of the well-mannered is discounted as dishonesty and insincerity. According to this conception, the ideal honest man would necessarily be uncouth, lacking in all self-control and restraint.

Prayer should conform to reality rather than to moods

This sham honesty appears in an especially grotesque form when it touches on man's relation to God. How often do we now hear such remarks on the Liturgy as: Why should I pray the *Confiteor* when I do not feel contrition? Why should I accuse myself of sins when I feel quite innocent, when I have not the slightest consciousness of sinfulness? How can I pray "Out of the depths I cry unto you, O Lord"[57] when I feel quite jolly?

The answer, of course, is that my prayers to God should conform to objective reality and not to my accidental mood. I know that in reality I am sinful. I know, consequently, that I should feel contrition. This objective reality is the measure of the wording of my prayers to God.

The liturgical theme is the conformity of my prayers to the objective situation of man before God and therefore to what I should experience in such a confrontation. Here, the choice of words ought not to depend on my feelings of the moment. The words are meaningful because they correspond to my true situation, to what I should be experiencing.

The words are the objective expression of attitudes which should form me and into which I should want to grow. Not honesty, therefore, but the nadir of sham honesty is revealed in the man who, misunderstanding the very purpose of prayer (or, indeed, of any cultic act), proudly refuses to utter words that do not reflect his momentary mood. In taking his accidental moods as the only valid norm he will follow, he betrays his self-centeredness and petty defiance.

The error here goes much further still. In the Liturgy we participate in the prayer of Christ and of His Church. This prayer is intended to form our souls, not to express our individual limitedness. It is moreover a prayer spoken out of a spirit of communion with all brethren. Hence, even if my own soul is filled with joy at a given moment, I can pray with the knowledge that many other persons are suffering and mourning; I know that the earth is a valley of tears. I have many a good reason, therefore, to pray the

[57] Ps. 129:1 (RSV = Ps. 130:1).

De Profundis even if I happen to feel only grateful joy for some great gift, or to pray a psalm of praise and thanksgiving while I am undergoing a great trial. Many of the very persons who seek to extol the Liturgy at the expense of private prayer because the latter allegedly does not promote communion among men seem to have missed this profound community aspect of liturgical prayer.

Modern philosophy is not particularly honest intellectually

Our epoch is as little deserving of special praise for its intellectual honesty as it is for its moral honesty.

Formerly, skeptics and relativists openly denied the existence of objective truth. But the attack on truth by the flourishing historical relativists of our own day takes on a more refined and covert form. Instead of openly denying truth they purport to "reinterpret" the whole notion of truth, but they end in the same wasteland of skepticism. This is hardly progress in the direction of greater intellectual honesty.

Similarly, if we compare the contemporary attacks on religion with those of, say, Voltaire and Renan, abominable as their mentality was, we must observe that former times were more honest and forthright. The modern debunkers try to convey the impression that theirs is a much more friendly approach, but by giving "new interpretations" to Christian truth and blurring the distinction between revelation and myth, they would dissolve the very essence of Christian faith.

Moreover, there is a fashion in philosophy today that tries to create the impression of depth by an overcomplicated rhetoric which frequently conceals a total lack of meaning. It solves the classical problems of philosophy by wordplay with newly invented terms, or by declaring that the problems are stupidly posed, or do not exist, or are unimportant. Is this a sign of intellectual honesty?

To compare several fashionable modern philosophers to Plato, Aristotle, St. Augustine, St. Thomas, and Descartes is to be forced to the conclusion that many of our "great" intellects are incomparably less honest than the thinkers of former times.

Reductionism is not honesty

There are other, more straightforward intellectual trends in our time that purport to lay bare honestly the reality that has been obscured by "unrealistic" traditions. For example, the positivist mentality in its various aspects considers the reality of a being to be in inverse proportion to its metaphysical rank. We think of those who, like Freud, try to reduce every spiritual entity to something that is not spiritual, who try to convince us that the most intellectual processes can be reduced to non-rational associations, that love is really nothing but sex and moral values are nothing but superstition.

The disillusionment these men wish to induce in the "unrealistic" man — that is, the man not yet exposed to their doctrine — is supposed to lead to realism and intellectual honesty. They regard themselves as very honest when they declare only the lower part of the universe to be real, as they reduce all spiritual relations and all motivation to mechanical processes, as they strip the universe of its spiritual content, as they debunk all objective values. Have they not presented a realistic version of the world? Have they not freed others from their illusions?

But if the reduction of the universe that they accomplish happens to be erroneous, it makes no sense to praise them for their remarkable honesty. And in fact, their conclusions are neither scientific nor philosophic, but superstitious. Their whole doctrine rests on a denial of what experience shows things to be. They claim that they are "getting behind" the thing to discover what it "really is." The superstitious man always professes to go behind the simple things of experience to read their "true import."

If we consider the psychological sources of this seeing everything *à la baisse* — this pseudo-realistic denial of the spiritual universe — it will be clear that pride and spiritual laziness are at its root. There is a peculiar obstinacy in approaching a being in a manner so out of harmony with the nature of the thing in question that the project is doomed to failure. It is as if these modern realists insisted on hearing colors and seeing sounds. Such men refuse to cooperate with the nature of reality.

One cannot consider such prejudice honest; rather, one should recall that there is a kind of intellectual dishonesty in every prejudice masquerading as philosophy or science. We should reserve our praise for the truly honest man who admits the full reality of the spiritual universe and is not intimidated by the intellectual fashions of the day.

Sham honesty infects even the Church

We have previously referred to the dilettante chatter that passes for thought in the ranks of many lay Catholic theologians who have been irresponsibly appointed to various Catholic colleges. Their insipid discussions about God and the world, about whether God still fits our society, whether we still "need" Him, are proof not only of the low level of their intelligence, but also of their dishonesty.

When they treat, in the most trivial way and from points of view that are totally unsuitable, questions of ultimate importance which have preoccupied men throughout history, they reveal an adolescent exhibitionism and pride. The slightest degree of honesty would make them aware of the total lack of sense in their approach.

We certainly do not mean to deny that many other very different trends are to be found in our epoch. But there is no doubt that progressive Catholics are recommending to the Church for Her blessing, support, and emulation intellectual attitudes that are characterized chiefly by a sham honesty.

16

Temporal parochialism

INCESSANTLY WE HEAR today the self-satisfied slogan, "Man has finally come of age." Yet there are so many features of the present epoch — the dethronement of truth by historical relativism, the fetishization of science, the devastation of our lives as a result of the laboratory view, and many others — that make it more than doubtful that modern man has really and truly *come of age*. There is, moreover, something inherently self-deceptive in the very idea.

Man has not "come of age" in the modern era

It is a characteristic symptom of immaturity to feel oneself more mature and independent than men of previous times, to forget what one owes the past, and, in a kind of adolescent self-assertion, to refuse any assistance. One need only recall Dostoyevsky's masterly description of the puberty crisis — Kolya Krassotkin in *The Brothers Karamazov*, Hypolit in *The Idiot*, the hero of *The Adolescent* — to grasp the special immaturity of the man who is convinced of his superior maturity, who thinks that in him humanity has in a unique way come of age, who is dominated by one preoccupation — to show his independence. His ludicrous smallness is manifest as he looks down on everything passed on through tradition, even the most timeless values.

The illusion of an historic coming of age is not the exclusive possession of our epoch. In the period of the so-called Enlightenment, men also felt themselves to have come of age and looked down on former times as periods of darkness and immaturity.

This illusion is a recurring phenomenon in social history and it bears a striking resemblance to the puberty crisis in the life of the individual person. But the contemporary assertion that whereas this perennial boast was never before justified, it is *now* really true makes its self-serving character all the more clear.

One of the many indications of the intellectual and moral immaturity of the present age is the fact that the percentage of worthless books and articles that captivate the minds of intellectuals seems greater today than in any other time in history.

Religious discussion also suffers from immaturity

Unfortunately, religious topics are not excluded from this inanity. Much of the discussion of the so-called "God is dead" movement is on the same level as Hitler's use of the term *God*. An Italian professor once told me of a conversation he had with Hitler. When he asked Hitler what he objected to in Communism, he said: "What I object to is that these people are atheists." He then began to shout: "Nothing is worse than a people who no longer believe in God." But when the professor asked him if by *God*, he meant a personal God, Hitler replied, "I would rather not answer that question."

The reason, of course, was that he did not mean anything by *God*; the word was just a weapon he employed to impress the

Catholic professor. Much of what passes for theological discussion nowadays is no less insincere. And the absurdity is compounded by our modern debunkers' claim that it is something new — but it is really old stuff, ideas that can be found in Voltaire, Feuerbach, Comte, Nietzsche, and others. The only thing new is the incomparably low intellectual and cultural level of these books and their absolute lack of originality. The intellectual midgets who write them remind one of the prophetic words of Kierkegaard: "Having refused to use their freedom of thought, men claim freedom of speech as compensation."[58]

Slogans now frequently replace thought

Another symptom of the immaturity of our age is the increased reliance on slogans. Once, slogans were largely restricted to enkindling mass enthusiasm in the political area. Today people are becoming more and more subject to slogans in all fields. Slogans are increasingly substituted for arguments and proofs. This constitutes a serious intellectual deterioration, for effective slogans are one of the greatest enemies of wisdom and truth. They are attractive to intellectuals just because they favor men's intellectual inertia and give them the opportunity of classifying things without having to engage in the labor of understanding their true nature.

One must marvel at the efficacy of slogans for all kinds of propaganda. National Socialist propaganda was filled with slogans and Communism used them with great success. Everyone is familiar with the way the terms *colonialism* and *imperialism* have been applied indiscriminately in order to discredit various countries. They are effective even when uttered with obvious insincerity by

[58] From an 1838 journal entry as quoted in Robert Bretall, ed., A *Kierkegaard Anthology* (Princeton, N.J.: Princeton University Press, 1946), 10.

spokesmen for Communist states that enslave their own citizens more ruthlessly than any European power governed its overseas colonies. In all this, Hitler's advice to "keep on repeating a lie until it is believed" is the governing principle.

These slogans acquire a mysterious sway over people and stimulate reactions of guilt or hostility independently of their truth or falsity. Many a man will swallow any nonsense just so he can be counted a "modern man," a "progressive," one who has "come of age." The spell of these slogans is all the more astonishing in view of the fact that their meaning is completely vague and oscillating. The prophets of tomorrow are quickly outdated. The progressives of yesterday are today's "reactionaries." We can have no doubt that a similar fate awaits our contemporary progressives.

The present age considers itself superior to the past

There is a special kind of pride in the idolatry of one's epoch. It produces a spirit of irreverence toward all tradition. It destroys philosophical inquiry because the notion of truth is replaced by that of *up-to-dateness*. This pride is similar to that which manifests itself as idolatry of one's nation, which we call *nationalism*. And just as the glory and might (real or supposed) of one's nation may compensate a man for the sense of his own inferiority, so too the real or supposed achievements of a man's epoch are used to compensate him for his insecurity and to nourish his pride.

This temporal parochialism — this feeling above others who are not living in the same historical epoch — performs the same psychological function that pride in Aryan descent performed for many Germans during the National Socialist epoch. The most insignificant German, suddenly exalted by the mere fact that he was of pure Aryan descent, could now look down on the most gifted intellectual who happened to have a Jewish grandmother.

There is a general tendency in human nature to seek such compensations for inferiority or to look for ways of "putting oneself up" in pride. And the alleged or real glory of the national (geographic) or temporal community to which one belongs lends itself marvelously to this function.

This epochalism existed in former times just as did nationalism, yet the revolt against tradition is especially strong today. And there are no objective reasons either for these optimistic expectations for the future or for this exaltation of the historical status of this age of relativism, dehumanization, and depersonalization.

Part III

The Secularization of Christianity

17

The fallacy of homogeneous historical periods

BEFORE WE DISCUSS the attitude the progressive Catholics have adopted toward the dangers of our own epoch, we must first deal with a widespread error of a more general nature. This is the conviction — frequently disavowed, but just as frequently evidenced in practice — that any given epoch in history is a closed entity characterized by an all-pervasive mentality. This is a great oversimplification.

Historical periods are not internally homogeneous

In fact, every epoch contains individuals who are in no way typical of their time, who have a completely different mentality and outlook from most of their contemporaries, as well as intellectual trends that are often quite antagonistic to one another.

Some sociologists and historians would interpret this very antagonism as stamping an age with a homogeneous character. They would hold that the issue at stake — for example, the question of human freedom — is constitutive of a given epoch and the fact that we can find contradictory opinions on this issue betrays the dependence of all on the themes presented them by their epoch. But this is a strained attempt to save the artificial theory of the homogeneous epoch.

The controversy may well have been important in various epochs. This is certainly true of the theme of freedom. And in one and the same epoch we can find juxtaposed trends implying radically different interests and mentalities. The oversimplified historiography behind the notion of the closed historical epoch just will not bear analysis.

Man remains the same throughout history

Related to this error is the exaggeration of the difference between one epoch and another. However different times may be in the external conditions of life, man himself remains basically the same. The state of technology and medicine and the organization of community life are very different today from what they were in the Middle Ages; but the sources of authentic happiness on earth remain the same: love, truth, marriage, family, creative work, and the beauty of nature and art. Though the changes in history bring many new problems, the same basic metaphysical controversies can be found in different epochs, and the same dramas of life.

It is indeed true that one can find in history the rise and fall of styles of life which characterize men's existence for a time and which find their expression in architecture, in customs, and in fashions of thought and behavior.

But essentially man does not change. Man remains exposed to the same moral dangers. He is in all ages equally in need of redemption, and he is equally called to moral perfection and even to sanctity. To him the words of St. Augustine still apply: "Thou hast made us for Thyself, O Lord, and our hearts are restless till they rest in Thee."[59]

Individual men differ profoundly within an era

Moreover, when it comes to profound and basic human questions, the difference between contemporaries can be, and often is, greater than the difference between men widely separated in time. The difference between Socrates and Callicles, as represented in Plato's *Gorgias*, is much greater than the difference between Callicles and Nietzsche. Beethoven and Rossini are much further apart than Beethoven and Bach. Michelangelo differs from his contemporary Bandinelli much more than he differs from Phidias. Cardinal Newman is immeasurably closer to St. Augustine than to Karl Marx. A greater distance separates Don Bosco from Garibaldi or Comte than from St. Francis of Assisi or St. Martin of Tours. The differences we speak of refer not only to the realm of ideas, but to the whole spiritual orbit in which these people moved.

There is no such universal as *modern man*

Terms such as *nineteenth century man* or *modern man* are ambiguous. No such universals exist; there are only intellectual and cultural trends that have a transitory dominance. The idea of modern man as a norm to which we all should conform is either deceitful or meaningless. Even if understood only as the bearer of a temporarily prevalent mentality, modern man can never be a norm for us. This "epochal" mentality can be in harmony or disharmony with truth, good or evil, deep or superficial.

[59] *Confessions*, Bk. 1, Ch. 1.

The mere fact that it is prevalent in a given historical epoch is no clue as to what attitudes we should take toward it. It may be that we should encourage and favor it; it may be that we should fight it with all our strength. Only if this mentality is good and grounded in truth should we favor it. In such a case it should be favored because of its inherent value apart from its socio-historical vitality and its temporary dominance.

To impose this mentality on all those who do not share it is obviously against the spirit of freedom and the respect for the dignity of the person and violates a fundamental principle of true democracy — respect for minorities. It is furthermore an absurd contradiction to decree arbitrarily (as so many intellectuals do) what modern man is and then claim that this is the norm of the epoch to which others who also live in the epoch must now conform. In fact, they puff themselves up in projecting their own mentality into the alleged modern man.

Morality and holiness do not change with the times

What is most important, however, is to see that the unity of style an epoch may have never entitles us to extend it to the sphere of truth and morality. It is impossible to speak of a Renaissance, a Baroque, or a modern truth, or of a Medieval and a modern morality, when by *morality* we mean the true nature of moral attitudes and not moral substitutes — which may indeed be typical of a certain epoch. All the more must this be said of religious matters. There is no Medieval holiness in contradistinction to a Baroque one, no holiness of the nineteenth century as distinguished from that of the twentieth.

Transformation in Christ is always essentially the same. The differences we find among saints is due much more to their different personalities than to the epoch in which they lived. And if one speaks of the piety typical of a certain epoch (always with the danger of oversimplification), this can only properly refer to a type of piety that does not contradict the piety of another epoch, but rather completes it. As long as we refer to an authentic Christian piety and not to deviations, the difference is similar to that which obtains between types of devotion — for example, the devotion to the Infant Jesus, the suffering Christ, or the Sacred Heart.

History has no univocal movement in one direction

The conception of homogeneous epochs is closely related to another false assumption — namely, that there is an immanent logic to the course of history, of which we can have certain knowledge. We have already discussed the errors of evolutionalism, progressivism, and the Hegelian dialectic. It is false to say that the sequence of historical epochs is characterized by a univocal movement in one and the same direction, whether good or bad. The evidence is that one period may be much more similar to a remote epoch than to an antecedent one. The Hegelian theory of the *Weltgeist* (World-Spirit) has no basis in fact. Challenging and brilliant as it may be, much as it reflects Hegel's genius, this theory remains mere speculation marked by naturalistic immanentism. Consequently (and notwithstanding Hegel's claims to the contrary), it is completely incompatible with Christian revelation.

Today's trends may be reversed tomorrow

When progressive Catholics ask the Church to adapt herself to the modern world, they usually indicate that what is at stake is the future world. They refuse to face up to the fact that there is not the slightest assurance that the currents and trends of today will not provoke a violent reaction tomorrow. There may be a strong reaction to the computer ideal, a strong reaction to the present amoralism, to the contemporary fashions in philosophy and art. These reactions do not, of course, have to come; but there is no excuse for ignoring the manifest possibility, if not the probability. The rationalism of the Enlightenment was followed by romanticism. History abounds in such examples.

The claim of the partisans of progressivism that the future belongs to them is totally unwarranted. It represents only an act of faith supported neither by science, philosophy, history, or revelation. It would be absurd and futile and a betrayal of Her mission for the Church to attempt to adapt Herself to the modern age, to the "future." As Pope John XXIII has said: The Church must give Her imprint to the nations and historical epochs, and not the reverse. Revelation addresses itself to the man of all ages — the essential human person whose unchanging nature alone entitles us to speak of man in general.

If a person endorses the idea of the homogeneous character of historical epochs and overrates the differences between various epochs, he will be gripped by the illusory notion that the man of our own age can only be reached with the message of Christ in a completely new way. His dilettantish interpretation of the *Kairos*, his preoccupation with reaching the "man of our age," will keep him from reaching the man of all ages.

Historical fatalism forgets man's free will

The facile notions that historical periods are intellectually and psychologically consistent and that there is an immanent logic in history lead to the belief that history is removed from our influence. However much truth there may be in this idea as far as technological development is concerned, it makes no sense when applied to ideologies and political systems. Many in Germany believed that National Socialism was inevitable, that its advent was independent of whether one wanted it or not. We frequently hear an analogous claim today on behalf of Marxism or some form of collectivism.

The Church is advised therefore to be wise and concern herself with surviving in a Communist world. This fatalism about history does not take into account man's freedom of will, his capacity to oppose a seemingly inevitable trend and to overcome it, or, indeed, the historical record itself. It is a Hegelian construct which leads again to a misinterpretation of the *Kairos*.

Christ alone has changed history essentially

We wish to repeat emphatically: there is no closed, homogeneous epoch in history; there is no "modern man." And most important of all, man always remains the same in his essential structure, in his destiny, in his potentialities, in his desires, and in his moral dangers; and this is true notwithstanding all the changes that take place in the external conditions of his life.

There is and has been but one essential historical change in the metaphysical and moral situation of man: the advent of Christ and the salvation of mankind and reconciliation with God through Christ's death on the Cross.

18

Fear of the sacred

LIKE A BESIEGED CITY, the Church is surrounded by the errors and dangers of our time. Unfortunately, some Catholics are not only not aware of these dangers, but are in varying degrees infected by them.

Overreaction to past errors can lead to new ones

There are certain theologians who are fighting against the intrusions of relativism, amoralism, and the laboratory approach to human life. They reject anything that seems to them to undermine genuine faith in Christ and the immutable doctrines of the Church. Yet their reaction against the faults of former epochs — such as legalism, ossification, and the abuse of authority — is so strong that they tend to overlook the dangers of our own time. It is always difficult to keep ourselves free from an unjustified optimism when we are full of joy over our liberation from certain evils, especially when these evils have weighed heavily upon our own lives. We will similarly direct our attention toward avoiding those faults which characterized our own behavior in the past, rather than equally or more serious faults which represent an opposite extreme. In fact, what often takes place is the kind of false reaction we discussed in Part I.

There is no doubt that much damage was done the Church in the past by a hard legalism and by a kind of pontificalism. Certain prelates exhibited an esotericism in the conduct of their office. There is no doubt that in spite of the voice of the Popes — for example, *Rerum Novarum* of Leo XIII — some priests and bishops were more interested in having good relations with the rich and powerful, or at least exhibited a greater solidarity with the "*bien pensants*,"[60] than with the workers or peasants. They sometimes showed little concern for the griefs of the poor.

But these unfortunate faults, which were counterbalanced by admirable expressions of Christian charity and heroic apostolic work, in no way justify the resentment against the upper strata of society and the spirit of class hatred and rivalry that are infecting elements of the clergy today, especially in France. Michel de St. Pierre has shown this fact in his two works *The New Priests* and *Sainte Colère.*[61] In some cases these reactions have reached the extreme of open flirtation with Marxism. This amounts to nothing less than a secularist apostasy.

We are speaking here of those theologians and others who oppose secularization, relativism, and naturalism but who yet, through an unguarded optimism, are in danger of ignoring and succumbing to the dangers of our time. There are no doubt some unconscious tendencies at work here. The legitimate antipathy to all esotericism and to all clerical condescension toward the layman

[60] The self-appointed "elite."

[61] *The New Priests* (St. Louis: Herder, 1966); *Sainte Colère* (Paris: Editions de La Table Ronde, 1965).

— especially if he belongs to the lower classes — has resulted in a great many cases in an unfortunate alliance with an idol of equality which seeks to destroy all hierarchical structures.

Sacredness is often falsely equated with elitism

In their fear of esotericism or prelatism, many priests today see the most valuable cultural features of the Church — such as the atmosphere of sacredness in the Liturgy — as an esoteric withdrawal from the simple man. They smell everywhere a neglect of the man in the street, an unchristian aristocraticism. And to a certain degree, they extend this suspicion to hierarchical structure in general. This antipathy against pontificalism tends to make them blind to the grave danger of self-indulgence and above all to the process of desacralization that characterizes our modern world. They seem to be unaware of the elementary importance of sacredness in religion.[62] Thus, they dull the sense of the sacred and thereby undermine true religion.

All men yearn for the sacred

Their "democratic" approach makes them overlook the fact that in all men who have a longing for God there is also a longing for the sacred and a sense of the difference between the sacred and the profane.

The worker or peasant has this sense as much as any intellectual. If he is a Catholic, he will desire to find a sacred atmosphere in the Church, and this remains true whether the world is urban and industrial or not. He will be able to distinguish the esoteric "above" from the divine "above." In no way will he resent the fact

62 This is manifested in the introduction of guitar and even jazz masses.

that God is infinitely above him, that Christ is the God-man. He looks joyfully upon the Church with Her divine authority. He expects every priest, as a representative of the Church, to emanate an atmosphere other than that of the average layman.

Functionalism never satisfies our longing for the sacred

Many priests believe that replacing the sacred atmosphere (that reigns, for example, in the marvelous churches of the Middle Ages or the Baroque epoch, and in which the Latin Mass was celebrated) with a profane, functionalist, neutral, and even humdrum atmosphere will enable the Church to encounter the simple man in charity. But this is a fundamental error. It will not fulfill his deepest longing; it will merely offer him stones for bread. Instead of combatting the irreverence so widespread today, these priests are actually helping to propagate this irreverence. They do not understand that esoteric pontificalism is really a form of secularization[63] and that its true antithesis is holy unction, which all the saints possessed — the spirit of reverence, the fusion of humility with a demeanor appropriate to the sacred office.

Holiness will attract men to Christ

Experience will tell everyone who has eyes to see and ears to hear that one saintly priest attracts more souls to Christ, especially from among "simple men," than do those who try to come nearer to the people by adopting an attitude that lacks the imprint of their sacred office. Michel de Saint Pierre has shown this fact admirably in his novel *The New Priests*. These priests do not speak to man's profoundest center. In merely reacting against a former

[63] See Chapter 5.

pontificalism they appeal only on a superficial, secular level. They may have some temporary success in attracting more people to church, in increasing parish activity. But they will not bring people closer to Christ, nor will they quench their deep thirst for God and for the peace that the world cannot give, that Christ alone can give.

The *Kairos* calls us to attract people to Christ, not merely to the parish. As Urs von Balthasar puts it: "The fantasy of the clergy is absorbed with the preoccupation of filling the time in the most useful and varied way. . . . The pastor is satisfied with the parish community because it has bravely participated in the service. The parishioners are satisfied with themselves. . . . It is a clear case of the Church being satisfied with herself."[64]

A false supernaturalism affects many clergy today

Those who confuse holy reserve with pontificalism and sacredness with esotericism exhibit a peculiar contradiction. They stress openness to the trends of our epoch, the elimination of an alleged aloofness in the former Christian conception of life, the bringing of religion as close as possible to everyday life. At the same time, they ignore the most basic features of human nature and thus fall into a false supernaturalism. For example, in an Ascension Day sermon, I heard a priest say that the Apostles' minds were clouded when they allowed themselves to be filled with sorrow over our Lord's departure. For, he reasoned, Christ is present in the midst of those who are gathered together in His name.

This argument overlooks the plain human fact that seeing is still more blissful than believing. Although on earth our relation

[64] Hans Urs von Balthasar, *Wer ist ein Christ?*, 4th edition (Zurich: Benziger, 1966), 38.

to Christ is based on faith which enables us to know that He is present in the Eucharist and in the midst of the faithful, everyone who truly loves Christ ardently nevertheless desires to see Him face to face in eternity. And every real Christian fully perceives the unheard-of privilege granted to the Apostles and disciples of enjoying the presence of Jesus, of being allowed to see Him, to listen to His words, to live in an actual communion with Him. Apart from mystical experience, this privilege cannot be replaced by any communion based only on faith. This deep longing for the fully experienced union with Christ, for the vision of Christ, pervades the lives of the saints. It resounds in the words of St. John at the end of the Apocalypse: "Come, Lord Jesus!"

It is expressed in the last verse of the wonderful *Adoro Te* of Thomas Aquinas:

> Jesus, whom now I look upon veiled,
> I pray, that what I long for so greatly may come to pass,
> That, gazing upon you with your face unveiled,
> I may be blessed with the sight of your glory.[65]

Love of neighbor is not love of Christ

There is a similar denial of human nature and a correlative supernaturalism in those who overemphasize Christ's presence in our neighbor and claim that it matters little whether we direct ourselves to Jesus Christ Himself or encounter Him in our neighbor. True as it is that we should find Christ in our neighbor, there is nevertheless a vast distance between our communion with

[65] *Jesu, quem velatum nunc aspicio,*
Oro, fiat illud, quod tam sitio:
Ut, te revelata cernens facie,
Visu sim beatus tuae gloriae.

Christ Himself and our finding Him in our neighbor. To be united in a direct *I-Thou* communion with Jesus Christ, the Infinitely Holy One, should be the great longing of our lives, the beatitude we are hoping for. To place finding Christ in our neighbor — even in the most insignificant or evil man — on the same level with our direct communion with Him is to misunderstand both human nature and Christian experience. In the first place there is a radical difference between the way in which a saint reflects Christ and the way in which He is found in any average person. The saints radiate something of Christ's holiness. We then can directly taste the very quality of holiness. But seeing Christ in lesser men results from sheer faith.

Moreover, as we have said, finding Christ in our neighbor necessarily presupposes a direct relation with Christ Himself. It is only because Christ has said, "What you have done to the least of my brethren, you have done to me,"[66] that we are able to find Christ in our neighbor in spite of all the obstacles which our neighbor may place in our path. And it is too often forgotten that Christ's words refer to our actions toward our neighbor, and not to the unique blissful experience — the *frui* — of the love communion with Christ. It may perhaps be arguable that actions done to our neighbor are literally done to Christ. But it is impossible to maintain that our beatitude is accomplished as much in communion with our neighbor as with Christ. The encountering of Christ in our neighbor is a feat of charity, and charity, we repeat, constitutes itself in the direct *I-Thou* communion with Christ.[67]

[66] Matt. 25:40.

[67] See Chapter 5.

19

Immanentist corruptions

THIS SECULARIZATION — this pseudo-*aggiornamento* — of Christianity reaches a much greater pitch of intensity in those intellectuals (priests and laymen) who are infected with various forms of secularist immanentism which are destructive of all true Christian faith.

Teilhardism embodies many modern errors

In the forefront of the immanentist ranks are the adherents of the ideas of Teilhard de Chardin. Even many who do not fully accept his "theology fiction" (as Etienne Gilson has called Teilhard's gnostic interpretation of Christian revelation) are under the influence of his replacing eternity with the historical future, his undermining of the difference between soul and body, spirit and matter, and his subsuming moral good and evil, holiness and sin, under different stages of evolution. It should not be necessary to insist on the absolute incompatibility of these views and Christian revelation. In Teilhard's gnostic "Christogenesis," there is no place for original sin, for the need of redemption, and, consequently, no place for the redemption of the world through Christ's death on the Cross. In this modern gnosis, Jesus Christ is not the God-man who brings the good tidings to men; He is not the epiphany of God who attracts men by His infinite holiness. He becomes instead an impersonal force, the initiator and the terminus of a process of cosmic evolution. Transformation in Christ is replaced by a human evolution that takes place over man's head, independently of his free decision. Instead of the resurrection of the body at the Last Judgment, Teilhard offers an identification of matter and spirit as the endpoint of evolution. Instead of the beatific vision — the eternal love-communion of the person with God — he promises the merging of individual consciousness in the general consciousness of a "superhumanity."[68]

That Teilhard's theology fiction embodies many of the typical contemporary intellectual perversions cannot be denied. There is first of all evolutionalism and progressivism. Second, there is a yielding to historical relativism, in that truth — even revealed truth — is made dependent on the "spirit of the age." We need only recall his argument that we can no longer expect men living in the scientific and industrial age to believe what has constituted the faith for two thousand years of Christian life. Third, there is a surrender to materialism in that the essential distinction between soul and body, spirit and matter, is obscured. And above all, Teilhard gives in to modern naturalism by eliminating the difference between nature and super-nature.

Closely linked to Teilhard's immanentism is his tendency to lose sight of the marvel of personal being, which implies a discrediting of individual existence as limited and imperfect in favor

[68] This is true as a general tendency, in spite of certain of his assertions to the contrary. For a fuller treatment of Teilhard, see the Appendix.

of the cosmic power of impersonal forces. This tendency toward a super-personal entity is the very opposite of, for example, Pascal's vision of the grandeur of man.

Pseudo-personalism rejects principles

In contrast, another contemporary trend exalts the person at the expense of "impersonal" and "cold" principles. This is the attitude of the proponents of various brands of the "new morality." They misinterpret the notion and legitimate role of principles. The most absurd expression of this misinterpretation is found in Fletcher's *Situation Ethics*.[69] This misinterpretation of principles permeates the ideas of many progressive Catholics, although in a less superficial form. It appears especially in their distinction between "Greek truth" and "personal truth" in Christ, a topic we consider in the next chapter. These Catholics assert that Christ's words, "I am the Truth,"[70] embody a superior notion of truth, not predicated of propositions but of a person. They emphasize the person as opposed to abstractions, and attack "abstract truth" — "principles" — in order to erect a "personal truth."[71]

Demythologization belittles historical truths of salvation

Sometimes these opposed tendencies (the Teilhardian annihilation and the "situationist" aggrandizement of the person) are joined. For example, Catholic followers of Bultmann claim that Christ did not come to inform us about supernatural truth but only to tell us to follow Him.

69 Joseph Fletcher, *Situation Ethics* (Philadelphia: Westminster Press, 1966).

70 John 14:6.

71 E.g., T. Sartory, G. Moran, and others infected by Bultmannism.

Astonishingly, Bultmann and his Catholic followers place no emphasis on the historical person of Jesus, but only on a kind of force or principle in men's souls. The contradiction is obvious. For those who stress the person against any proposition, the concrete individual reality of personal being against abstract principles — those who oppose the personal truth incarnated in Christ to any logical truth — would certainly be expected, therefore, to stress the historical, individual existence of the person of Christ. But it is just this concrete existence of the God-man that is belittled in the name of "demythologization."

This Bultmannian desire to demythologize the Gospels finds a strange bedfellow in the pseudo-existentialist antipathy to the meaning, dignity, and basic function of true propositions, of principles; for the entire trend of demythologization implies a belittling of the historical, concrete realities of the Gospel. Thus, principles are opposed on behalf of persons, and persons are deposed on behalf of the principle of demythologization.

The entire confusion has its source in Heidegger, whose influence on Bultmann and on many Catholic intellectuals is well known. Heidegger's denial of the subject-object situation means that there is also no room left for the "thou." As Gabriel Marcel rightly points out, the real "I" manifests itself only in communion with the "thou." Hence, the real, full dignity of the person — this unique and incomparable new dimension of being — is obscured in Heidegger, notwithstanding his stress on the superiority of *Dasein* (the human being) over *Seindes* (the pure existent).

Some theologians rationalize mystery and blur precise facts

Heideggerianism can be seen in the attempt of certain theologians to replace the mysteries revealed to us in the Gospel by an obscure and abstract metaphysics. This is especially apparent in their interpretation of the central mystery of the Incarnation. The Nicene Creed speaks with great simplicity and lucidity of this impenetrable mystery. The Jesuit Karl Rahner, on the contrary, replaces this mystery with obscure, abstract speculation: God asserts Himself in man, and everyone who accepts his creaturehood accomplishes something analogous to the Incarnation. Now, the fusion of univocal fact with absolute mystery is the very mark of revealed truth, but in Rahner's speculation, facts lose their preciseness and the mysteries are replaced by confusing rationalizations.

Furthermore, blurring the mysteries and substituting nebulous metaphysics for revealed and inscrutable truth blatantly contradicts the much trumpeted desire to bring religion close to the men of our time. The facts of revelation in all their lucid concreteness and impenetrable mystery have touched the souls of the simplest and the subtlest of men through two thousand years. But the murky metaphysics put forward to replace them — aside from the fact that it is neither the authentic message of Christ nor sound philosophy — can never mean anything to the non-intellectual.

It appears to us that these murky speculations result from an earnest desire on the part of these intellectuals who are called *progressive* to save as much as possible of a Christian faith that they are in danger of losing completely — that genuine Christian faith that we find unchanged through the centuries, whether in a St. Francis de Sales, a St. Thérèse of Lisieux, or a Curé of Ars. But this desperate attempt, earnest as it may be, is absolutely incompatible with the doctrine of the Holy Catholic Church.

Scientism strips the Gospel of the miraculous

The science fetishism discussed previously has also made its way among members of the Catholic Church. This is obvious in the case of Teilhard de Chardin. But many who are not attracted by Teilhard's gnosis nevertheless tacitly accept the identification of truth with "scientific" truth. This imposes on them the necessity of constructing some other notion of truth in order to save a place for Christian faith. The influence of science fetishism is determinative in the idea, so dear to many, that it is necessary to amend the Gospel so as to eliminate everything that is unpalatable to men living in the scientific age.[72]

As we indicated in Chapter 4, there can be no contradiction between revealed truth and science, but only between revealed truth and certain philosophical speculations, interpretations, deductions, or presuppositions that somehow become illegitimately associated with certain scientific discoveries.

The alleged incompatibility of science and the miracles related in the Gospels calls to mind a story a Franciscan told me some fifty years ago. A doctor told him that, as a physician, he obviously could not be expected to accept the virgin birth of Christ. The Franciscan retorted that to know that a virginal birth is normally impossible, one really does not have to be a scientist or a physician! Chesterton has a few words to say on this topic in *Orthodoxy*:

> An imbecile habit has arisen in modern controversy of saying that such and such a creed can be held in one age but cannot be held in another. Some dogma, we are told, was credible in the twelfth century, but is not credible in the twentieth. [But] what a man can believe depends upon his philosophy, not upon the clock or the century. If a man believes in unalterable natural law, he cannot believe in any miracle in any age. If a man believes in a will behind law, he can believe in any miracle in any age.[73]

[72] This is the case with Thomas Sartory.

[73] G. K. Chesterton, *Orthodoxy* (Garden City, N.Y.: Image, 1959), 74-75.

No one asks atheists to accept miracles. If, however, one believes in a personal, almighty God, creator of heaven and earth, it is ridiculous to suppose that scientific progress could preclude belief in miracles. Outstanding modern scientists such as Planck, Pasteur, Carrel, and countless others, were convinced Christians.

Faith is independent of the natural sciences

In fact, the degree of scientific knowledge available has no bearing on acceptance of Christ's revelation: faith always implies a leap transcending all natural knowledge. Did not St. Paul say that Christ was foolishness to the Greeks?[74] The gulf between the believer and the rationalist who rejects faith is found in all periods of history and the modern revolt against miracles and all manifestations of the supernatural is not new. Rousseau declared that if miracles were eliminated from the Gospel, he would adore Christ. The same spirit is found in Voltaire and the Encyclopedists.

As a response to God's revelation in the Old and New Testaments, faith implies a transcendence of what can be grasped with our reason, a transcendence of our natural knowledge. It is clear, therefore, that faith cannot be altered by any scientific development. Even philosophical insights are independent of the natural sciences; all the more can this be said of revealed truth.

Science is blind to the hierarchy of being

One frequently gets the impression that progressive Catholics consider serious and real only what the natural sciences endorse; they limit themselves to what we have called "a laboratory view of

[74] 1 Cor. 1:23.

the universe." In failing to understand that the human aspect of the world is fully valid, these persons become blind to the metaphysical depth and significance of such categories as "above" and "below."

The fact that there is no place in the universe of science for these notions in no way diminishes, or even affects, the reality of these categories, which are inevitably expressed in the spatial analogy "above" and "below." "Above" remains a fundamental symbol for the things that are metaphysically superior to us in virtue of their value and ontological rank; "below" stands for the things which are below the level of our human existence.

St. Paul's words, "Seek the things that are above,"[75] retain their full meaning for man, even if "above" and "below" cannot be found in the spatial universe. To lift one's eyes in prayer retains its justification, even if it is nonsensical to believe that God — He who is beyond all spatial determination — is literally "above the clouds." The deep and inalterable significance of these symbols has been perceptively expounded by Gabriel Marcel, and only an insipid mind could assume that they have lost their profound meaning because of the findings of natural science.[76]

Many moderns seem to have lost their faith

The spirit of many articles published in *America*, *Concilium*, *Commonweal*, and *Cross Currents*, as well as of many remarks made here and abroad, is such that one cannot escape the impression of an unwillingness in the authors any longer to accept faith in its full and authentic sense. Many seem to forget the essential

[75] Col. 3:1.

[76] Gabriel Marcel, *The Mystery of Being*, vol. 1, *Reflection and Mystery* (Chicago: Regnery, 1960), 49-51.

gesture of faith, which is something that completely transcends the world surrounding us and all natural knowledge. If we want to avoid the leap into the dark (a leap based on an overwhelmingly luminous datum) then real faith is no longer possible for us.

20

The sapping of truth

ENAMORED OF our present epoch, blind to all its characteristic dangers, intoxicated with everything modern, many Catholics no longer ask whether something is true, whether it is good and beautiful, or whether it has intrinsic value. They ask only whether it is up-to-date, suitable to modern man and the technological age, challenging, dynamic, audacious, or progressive.

Yet there is a tendency that is more refined than subordination of truth to the fashions of our time. This is the attempt to interpret the notion of truth in a way that saps its very content. This error is presented in an orthodox and religious guise and so is more dangerous to faith. We are referring to the distinction, gaining popularity, between "Greek" and "biblical" notions of truth.

It is a typical feature of our sociology-oriented age to present the most elementary data of human experience as deriving from the mentalities of certain nations and cultures.[77] This intellectual

[77] Cf. Father Bernard Lonergan, S.J., the address delivered at Marquette University, May 12, 1965. Similar ideas are developed in Thomas Sartory.

fashion becomes particularly absurd when applied to truth. The authentic notion of truth is in fact so fundamental and indispensable that even attempts to give it a "new" interpretation presuppose it. Truth is not a national, cultural, or epochal property.

Truth is the conformity of a statement to reality

Truth is the conformity of a statement to reality, to the existing facts. The entire emphasis here is laid on the fact that something is really thus and so. The sphere of being to which the statement refers may vary, but the test of its truth always remains the same. The proposition may refer to a general law, to an essential relation, or even to a concrete fact. But the statements, "Moral values presuppose persons" and "Napoleon died at St. Helena" do not differ in quantum truth, however much the realities referred to differ.

A true statement, whether in philosophy or empirical science, is one that possesses objective validity and is thus opposed to falsity, to the non-validity of an affirmed illusion or fiction. Moreover, the truth of a statement referring to a concrete fact — a so-called historical truth — does not differ from the truth of universal statements.

The source of its truth is the actual existence of the fact. To say there is a truth which has an historical stamp is therefore quite ambiguous. The reality to which the truth refers is, of course, an historical event. But the truth itself is not historical. That Napoleon died at St. Helena is true, was true fifty years ago, and will always be true. Thus, there is no "historical truth," only a truth about historical facts.

Even though truth is in the first instance predicated of a proposition, it remains completely focused on the existence of some being, whether a concrete fact or an ideal state of affairs. In other words, the very soul of truth is the existence of the being to which it refers. The question, "Is it so, or is it not?" is equivalent to the question, "Is it true, or is it not?" To see in truth something merely logical, something belonging merely to the conceptual order, is to miss its all-important existential impact.

"Greek truth" and "biblical truth" are not at odds

What decides the question of whether a statement is true or not is exclusively the reality of the being in question. Thus, we must realize that truth reaches as far as being does. Truth is the echo of being.

It is therefore absolutely wrong to create any antagonism between "Greek truth," which belongs to the sphere of propositions, and a "biblical truth," which is concerned with reality and being. The reference to being is indissolubly linked to truth, regardless of whether the being is of a metaphysical or an historical nature, whether the existence in question is a general idea or a concrete, individual fact. To every possible being there corresponds the truth of a potential statement about its existence or the nature of its existence.

There is nothing that is beyond the purview of truth, be it in the realm of our possible knowledge or outside of it, whether a mystery or something accessible to rational knowledge. Even the agnostic presupposes the existence of truth, though he declares that we cannot attain it. It should be clear that it is utterly ridiculous to interpret the most elementary fact, the most indispensable question of truth as a specialty of the Greek mind. In every question of daily life, whether of the most primitive person or the most sophisticated, truth is assumed. Whether we accuse a man of being a liar or whether we trust him, the question of truth continues to be taken for granted.

The truths of the faith are not merely historical

Allegedly, "Greek truth" differs from "biblical truth" not only because the former is philosophical and abstract while the latter is historical but also because Greek truth is coextensive with *knowledge* (ethical, metaphysical, or logical) whereas biblical truth concerns *faith*. The confusion generated here results from equating two basic distinctions: that between philosophical and historical truth, and that between truths of knowledge and truths of faith.

To claim that biblical truth — "faith" — refers exclusively to historical fact is certainly incorrect. Although history, indeed, plays a predominant role in the Old and New Testaments, many fundamental facts have no historical character and are nonetheless part of divine revelation. That Moses received the Decalogue on Mt. Sinai is an historical fact, but the content of that same Decalogue cannot be called historical. That God gave these commandments to man might be said to be historical, but their intrinsic goodness and universal applicability is certainly not. Christ's remark, "He who calls his brother 'fool' shall deserve the fire of Gehenna,"[78] is certainly not a historical truth. And in the statement, "He who believes will attain eternal life,"[79] we are again confronted with a general truth that applies to every human being. Thus, it is completely wrong to declare that the Bible, especially the New Testament, is concerned only with historical facts.

Historical truths are not less true than other kinds of truth

Certainly all the truths in the Bible, especially those of the New Testament, have an existential character, in the sense that

78 Matt. 5:22.

79 John 3:15.

Kierkegaard uses the term. They are all related to ultimate, divine reality and to the *unum necessarium*.

But this existential character cannot be expressed by saying, as do some theologians, that these truths have an historical coloration. This seems to imply — the term, of course, is ambiguous — that a truth which is historical is somehow less absolute than a non-historical truth, or that it is in some way dependent on the course of history.

Conviction and faith differ

There is a real distinction between knowledge and conviction, on the one hand, and divine revelation and faith, on the other. But in no sense does this distinction concern the notion of truth. Truth is always one and the same.

The distinction consists, rather, in the enormous disparity between those things which are in principle accessible to our reason and those other things, presented in divine revelation, which in principle surpass all possible rational understanding. Therefore, there will be a decisive difference between *faith* and *conviction* based on rational knowledge.

All truths have the same basic character as truth

The difference between the objects of "reason" and those of "faith" is obvious. But this difference has no consequence for the notion of truth. The Holy Trinity, the beatific vision, the resurrection of the body — each either exists or does not exist and the profession of these mysteries is either true or not. The sentence, "Christ rose from the dead," does not differ in quantum truth from any other true statement, however supremely incomparable it may be as a reality.

Faith in differs from *faith that*

We must see another important distinction when we consider faith and natural conviction. It does not imply a duality in truth, but it is vital in the realm of faith. This is the distinction between *faith in* and *faith that* made by Martin Buber and Gabriel Marcel.

Without any doubt, there is a decisive difference between, on the one hand, the act of surrendering to Christ, the response to the ineffable epiphany of God in the Sacred Humanity of Christ, and, on the other hand, our accepting a mystery which Christ reveals to us. The first act — the *faith in* — is the fundamental religious experience. It is the response of Abraham when he felt like dust and ashes in the confrontation with the absolute person and complete otherness of God, the mysterious, infinite superiority which Rudolf Otto describes in *The Idea of the Holy.*[80]

Faith in is a surrender to a person

This total, adoring giving ourselves up to the person of God is the *faith in.* We find it exemplified in many places in the Gospel, such as in the Apostles' response to the call of Christ and in the person who, when asked, "Dost thou believe?" fell down and adored Him.[81]

This act surpasses rational conviction; it is a specific surrender to a person. It occurs only in relation to a person. Even more, it must be a surrender to the Absolute Person, either to God (as it was in the case of Moses) or to the self-revealed God in Christ (as it was in the case of the Apostles). *Faith in* is not a theoretical

[80] Rudolf Otto, *The Idea of the Holy*, 2d ed. (New York: Oxford University Press, 1950).

[81] John 9:35-38.

response (such as the belief that something exists, the object of which is a state of facts) but an all-embracing act in which the person completely surrenders mind, will, and heart to the Absolute Person.

As a response to the Infinite Holiness of God, it calls for the giving up of all critical distance and all proving and testing. Yet it is simultaneously pervaded by the unshakable conviction that this response is due; and that it is the very opposite of being overwhelmed simply by the dynamism of something, the very opposite of being swamped and carried away by an irresistible passion or by a force which we experience as stronger than ourselves.

No, *faith in* is animated by the free sanction I have described in my book *Ethics*.[82] It is filled with the experience of a lived confrontation with the Incarnate Truth. Such was the experience of St. Paul on the way to Damascus and of Pascal as described in his famous document, *The Memorial*. Yet in every prayer to God there is a definite actualization of the *faith in*.

Faith that is conviction about a truth

Faith that is seen in our response to all the realities revealed by Christ. We believe that there is an eternal life, that our body will really rise, that our eternal salvation depends upon our following Christ; and we believe these things because Christ has revealed them to us. This faith is a definite theoretical response; its objects are states of fact and not persons. Different as it is from any merely rational conviction (for example, of a metaphysical truth based on knowledge), *faith that* is closer to it than is *faith in*; for the theme here is truth. The sayings of Christ are believed to be true.

[82] Chicago: Franciscan Herald Press, 1972.

Christianity involves *faith in* and *faith that*

Both *faith in* and *faith that* are involved in our Christian faith. *Faith in* is the very basis of *faith that*. Objectively, our *faith in* Christ is the foundation of our *belief that* what Christ has revealed is true. Moreover, *faith in* belongs to every fully religious life. There is, surely, a danger that many will accept religion purely as a matter of inheritance, in which case *faith that* will take precedence over *faith in*, and the latter may recede well into the background. But everyone who possesses a *faith in* always has a *faith that*, as well.

Truth is thematic in *faith in* and in *faith that*

The role of truth in *faith that* is obvious. It is apparent in the *Credo*. It would be nonsensical to claim (as Sartory and others do) that a person does not hold the content of his *faith that* to be real, authentic, and objectively valid. A believer must necessarily affirm that this content is true. But the theme of truth is also present in every act of *faith in*. A person who has faith in God inevitably also is convinced of the existence of God. A person who has faith in Christ is also firmly convinced that Christ is God. To every *faith in* there corresponds not only a *faith that* the revelations of God are true, but also a *faith that* the person in whom we have faith exists.

When, for example, we hear beautiful music and are deeply moved by it, our experience is certainly not a judgment about the beauty of the music. It is rather a direct contact with the beauty of the music, a being touched by the beauty, and a responding with enthusiasm. But without any doubt, the statement, "This music is beautiful," is implicitly held to be true. This is only a faint analogy, but it may suffice to suggest the manner in which every *faith in* implicitly contains a *faith that* the object of our faith exists.

The person in whom I believe, to whom I surrender, is the absolute one. I believe that He is God, the epiphany of God. Important as it is, therefore, to distinguish *faith in* from *faith that* — important as it is to see that the former is the very basis of the latter — it is impossible to separate them in a way that would suggest that *faith in* could ever exist without *faith that*. The two attitudes — the surrender to the person of Christ as God and the belief that Christ is the Son of God — are indeed different; but the *faith that* He is the Son of God is necessarily connected with the *faith in* Him. It is impossible for any faithful Christian not to believe that Christ is the Son of God. In Christ's question to his disciples ("Who do you say that I am?") and in St. Peter's answer ("Thou art the Christ, the Son of the Living God"), the *faith that* is clearly present.[83] And it is equally present in the sacerdotal prayer, "They have believed that Thou hast sent me."[84]

In both cases, let it be noted, the question of truth is fully present — truth, in the ultimate, all-embracing, inevitably presupposed meaning of the term. And this truth has no ambiguous "historical component."

We are called to live the truths of faith

It is also ambiguous to put forward the notion that biblical faith means that we follow Christ in our life. This is the thesis that Thomas Sartory puts forward amid all the confusion he generates in his playing with words. Now, it is certainly true that the living faith that Kierkegaard stresses implies our following Christ. Faith implies more than our conviction that what Christ has revealed is true; it implies a living of Christ in our soul, a continuously

[83] Matt. 16:15-16.

[84] John 11:42.

renewed giving of ourselves to Christ, and a seeing everything in the light of Him.

Lived faith is grounded in truth

But faith as such, which St. Paul clearly distinguishes from hope and charity, is nonetheless indissolubly connected with the conviction that Christ is the Son of God, the epiphany of God. In short, faith is connected with the Divinity of Christ. To deny this very core of faith (of *faith that*, as well as of *faith in*) is to annihilate the faith to which the Gospel continually refers. When truth in its authentic sense plays no role in faith, faith has been lost.

There is a glaring contradiction in the idea of Sartory and others that only faith in Christ and faithfulness to Him in our lives are absolute and that every proposition which expresses something implicit in our faith is subject to historical evolution. This is a mere playing with words, which, incidentally, has become quite a fashionable way of solving problems since Heidegger.

The saints are the great witnesses of Christ and of the redemption of the world through Christ's death on the Cross. They demonstrate the ineradicable connection of both *faith in* and *faith that* with the transformation of personality in Christ. They truly realize the words of St. Paul: "I live, yet not I, but Christ lives in me."[85] The lives of the saints exemplify the crucial importance of our following Christ, which includes love of God, love of neighbor, and dwelling in the paths of the Lord — in one word, realization of the totality of natural and supernatural morality.

Stress on this conforms fully to the doctrine of the Church and even finds its classical expression in the Catholic doctrine of

[85] Gal. 2:20.

justification which holds, against the Lutheran *sola fides* (faith alone) theory, that justification cannot be separated from sanctification and that only faith formed by charity (*fides caritate formata*) can lead to salvation.

Imitation of Christ presupposes belief in many truths

This true following of Christ presupposes not only such a *faith in*, but also *faith that* the Apostolic and Nicene Creeds are true. If it is erroneous to substitute the *sola fides* for the *fides caritate formata*, it is all the more so to substitute imitation of Christ for faith. For the very basis of the imitation of Christ is faith in Christ; and this commitment to Christ cannot be separated from the firm belief *that* God exists, and *that* Christ is the Son of the Living God.

This fact discloses the full thematicity of truth. Thus, we see that the "biblical faith" advocated by Thomas Sartory and others is a completely ambiguous notion and leads to hopeless confusion. His "biblical faith" is neither the real *faith in* nor the real imitation and commitment that we witness in the saints.

Truth has profound dignity and value

The whole dissolution of truth is epitomized in the answer once given by a theologian to the following question: "Did the Angel Gabriel really announce to the Virgin Mary the fact that she would give birth to Christ?" He answered, "This is an oriental truth." This answer implied that there are somehow different types of truth: an oriental and an occidental, an old and a new. His juggling with the notion of truth reminds one of the distinction made between Jewish and Aryan mathematics made by the president of the Association of Mathematicians in National Socialist Germany.

When St. Augustine says, "What does our soul desire more than truth?" or when he exclaims, "Oh truth, truth, how did the very marrow of my bones yearn for thee,"[86] he is obviously referring to something over and above the truth of fundamental statements. Truth is envisaged as a whole, as one — as when we speak of the *kingdom of truth*. Here, as in the expression, "Truth shall make us free,"[87] the dignity and value of truth flashes forth. In this notion of truth as the splendor of light against darkness, of purity against impurity, of univocity against ambiguity, of clarity and articulation against chaos, the full dignity of being against non-being is present. We encounter here an ultimate datum which reaches into unfathomable depth and mystery. We cannot pursue it in this work, but we may quote the following passage from Guardini:

> Plato must have had an extraordinary experience of truth. For him, it is not merely the adequacy of a proposition, but an experience of truth with all its sublime import and plenitude of significance that the undistorted truth implies. For Plato, truth is not only the correctness and clarity of an insight; it is that sublime value which transcends the concrete content in every genuine knowledge.[88]

We come closer to this notion of truth if we consider the different gradations of weight and depth which the truth of a statement can assume, depending on whether it is of an insignificant, accidental nature or an important one. The content of propositions differs in many ways: important or unimportant, deep or superficial, intrinsically necessary or purely empirical.

86 St. Augustine, *Confessions*, Bk. 3, Ch. 6.

87 Cf. John 8:32.

88 Romano Guardini, *Stationen und Rückblicke* (Würzburg: Werkbund, 1965).

Although, as we saw, differences in content do not entitle us to speak of different types of truth, a truth nevertheless assumes a weight, status, and splendor according to the rank of the being in question. The splendor of a truth involving values is immeasurably greater than one that only deals with a neutral fact.

The higher the fact to which a truth refers, the more we can grasp the glorious value of truth. And yet, in every truth, even that of the most modest sentence, there is a reflection, however faint, of the glory of truth.

Christ is the splendor of truth

It is in this light that we must understand Our Lord's words, "I am the Truth."[89] Here we encounter the one all-embracing truth, the kingdom of truth in all its liberating splendor — but in a completely new reality, which is truth as a person. The difference is analogous to that between justice and goodness and God's *being* infinite justice and goodness. The incomparably superior reality which personal being possesses over impersonal is here apparent. In Christ we are confronted with Incarnate Truth, the Incarnate Word, in whom the overwhelming glory of the truth has an ultimate personal reality. As the truth that redeems us, that makes us free, Christ draws us into the Kingdom of Truth.

Truth is the foundation of Christian faith

No twaddle about the difference between Greek and biblical truth can ever affect the fact that truth in all its dimensions is the backbone of Christian faith. Whether a person's faith is based on truth or error has an ultimate impact. In comparing the position

[89] John 14:6.

of men like Thomas Sartory with that of Cardinal Newman or of any saint of the past, we are forced to conclude that many of the progressive Catholics have in reality lost their faith and are now trying desperately, by confused and pretentious constructs, to deceive both themselves and others about this dread fact.

21

Amoralism

ONE OF THE MOST OMINOUS symptoms of decay in the Church today is the growing acceptance of modern amoralism. We do not mean that more immoral deeds are committed today than before but that blindness to moral values, an indifference to the question of moral good and evil, an acceptance of the superstition that good and evil are illusions or taboos, is one of the signs of the time.

Moderns deny the reality of good and evil

We are not concerned with alleged philosophers who deny the reality of the categories of moral good and evil. Such relativistic pseudo-philosophers have always existed. Rather, we are concerned with that distorted vision of life manifested in the growing tendency to approach the most terrible sins as if they were something completely neutral, like mere physiological processes or any event in the realm of impersonal nature.

Indeed, there have always been cynical persons with a diabolical antipathy to the world of moral values. But they did not consider the world of moral values as non-existent; they hated it and revolted against it in the manner of Cain. And there have always been very many persons who were affected with a partial moral blindness, such as Tom Jones with his blindness to the sin of impurity. But the category of moral good and evil remained operative in many other areas. What is new in our time, however, is the moral neutralization of the world through the elimination of the all-important categories of good and evil. And this new amoralism is taken to be progress, the result of our having come of age, a liberation from the fetters of traditional taboos.

Amoralism has a number of causes

It would be to go beyond the purpose of this book to broach an analysis of the causes of this deplorable decay. It will have to suffice to suggest the role that the laboratory view and the fetishization of science have played. Freudianism bears a special responsibility for this attitude. The irony in the belief that an amoral approach is more "objective," more "scientific," is dramatized by the fact that Freud's theories are filled with myths and fictions.[90] That Freud is accepted naively by many teachers in this country has been conducive to the elimination of the categories of good and evil in high school and college education.

Amoralism has infected Catholic thinking

Now this amoralistic superstition has invaded Catholic circles. In addition to the two chief causes mentioned above, we must here note two other reasons for the successful propagation of the spirit

[90] We do not deny that Freud has also made some valuable contributions.

of amoralism among Catholics: the revolt against obligations and the reaction against legalistic moralism.

I have analyzed the revolt against obligations (and the whole subject of situation ethics) in *Morality and Situation Ethics*.[91] It is closely connected with the wrong conception of freedom discussed previously and manifests itself in so-called situation ethics (sometimes incorrectly described as existentialist ethics). We are not thinking of Fletcher's unfortunate book, which is nothing more than an unearthing of Benthamite utilitarianism, but of the ethical trend in Catholic youth movements and in authors such as Graham Greene and Gertrud von le Fort.

Legalistic moralism may have provoked rejection of morals

The receptivity to amoralism can also be explained as a reaction against legalistic moralism which in the past resulted in a caricature of the glorious wealth and beauty of moral goodness. It reduced all morality to prohibitions, an attitude which a German humorist described in the following way: "The good is always the evil that one fails to do."

Unfortunately, this attitude was reflected in the discussions of marriage in many textbooks on moral theology. There was mainly an enumeration of what was forbidden, but nothing about the positive values that were at stake, the desecration of which is the source of the terrible sin of impurity. This legalistic presentation was accompanied by a failure to indicate the difference between supernatural and natural morality.

It was not only legalistic, negativistic moralism that brought about a reaction. It was also the fact that in the promulgation of

[91] Chicago: Franciscan Herald Press, 1966.

the word of God, moral prescriptions were emphasized much more than the great mysteries of Christ's redemption. The glory of supernatural morality was thereby obscured. Deplorable as these shortcomings were, the reaction in the direction of moral indifference is incomparably worse.

Morality is an essential element in Christianity

One could observe many amoralistic trends creeping into sermons some years before Vatican II. I once heard a sermon in which the preacher stressed that Christ did not come to bring moral prescriptions, but the Kingdom of God. Though the latter part of this proposition is certainly true, the assumption that morality plays no role in the institution of the Kingdom of God is a shocking error.

We must realize that it is an essential mark of Christian revelation that religion and morality are intimately and ultimately interwoven. The moral goodness and the awe-inspiring absoluteness of the divine are fused in a unique way in the datum of holiness. In the Sacred Humanity of Christ, this datum of holiness is revealed as something completely new, beyond all the ideals a human mind can form.

And yet this holiness is simultaneously the fulfillment and transfiguration of all natural morality.

Amoralism is a symptom of loss of faith

The amoralism gaining currency among Catholics is indeed one of the most alarming symptoms of a loss of authentic Christian faith. Goods such as the earthly welfare of mankind, scientific progress, and the domination of the forces of nature are either considered much more important than moral perfection and the avoidance of sin or at least evoke much greater interest and enthusiasm.[92]

Typical of this moral indifference were Fr. Karl Rahner's remarks during the dialogue with the Communists at Herrenchiemsee.[93] He indicated that many moral values may disappear in the future and only the dignity of the human person and some other values remain.

Now, the dignity of the person in the strict sense is not a moral value, but a morally relevant good. Man's dignity refers to the high ontological rank he possesses as a person. This dignity certainly imposes moral obligations on us, such as the necessity of respecting this dignity — of not abusing other persons, not infringing on their rights. But the value of this dignity is patently not a moral value. Man possesses this value by the very fact that he is created in the likeness of God. That a person of Father Rahner's stature could take such a relativistic attitude toward the moral sphere and consider ontological values alone immutable indicates the power that amoralism has gained in the Church.

It is as if the sense of the unique, intrinsic grandeur and importance of moral values had been lost by a great many progressive Catholics. They are not able to comprehend the whole glorious world which is at the center of Plato's thought and which in its supernatural transfiguration is at the center of the Gospel. They see morality as a rather petty, merely infrahuman affair which cannot be compared with the greatness of ontological perfections or the progress of humanity.

[92] This is manifest in Teilhard de Chardin's outlook. Similar ideas are expressed in the writings of Daniel Callahan and many other American progressive Catholics.

[93] Herder Correspondence, III (1966), 243-47.

As might be expected, the speculation of Teilhard de Chardin, that locus of so many contemporary errors, also provides theoretical support for amoralism. Father Teilhard replaces the moral question with an ontological growth resulting from evolution. Sin is viewed as merely a lower stage of evolution and virtue a higher one. The fundamental fact that sin alone offends God and supernatural virtue alone glorifies Him does not belong in Teilhard's depersonalized world.

Weak ethical arguments do not change morality

Some of the "new moralists" buttress their defiance of traditional Christian morality by pointing to deficiencies in former arguments for Christian morality. The Church might therefore be forced to alter Her understanding of the Christian virtues. A typical example of this error (which Marcel calls a *transaction frauduleuse*) is the Jesuit Father W. Molinsky's suggestion that the sinfulness of premarital intercourse (i.e., impurity) is now in doubt because the arguments St. Thomas brought for this sinfulness are weak.[94]

But does the fact that impurity is a sin depend on St. Thomas's arguments, which are indeed weak? Was not impurity clearly condemned as a sin in the Gospel and throughout the history of the Church prior to St. Thomas? Doubtless, traditional arguments offered for the moral value of a virtue and the moral disvalue of a sin are sometimes insufficient and should be replaced by valid arguments. This would constitute a progress in ethical insight. But it would not be the supplanting of an "old" by a "new" morality. The term *new morality* is misleading, because *morality* always refers

[94] Herder Correspondence, III (1966), 370.

to moral values and disvalues and not to their philosophical formulation. The latter is called ethics. There may be changes in Christian *ethics*, but never in Christian *morality*.

Morality is immutable

As we have had occasion to point out previously, the idea that a moral value or disvalue could change according to the spirit of the age is out of the question. Either something was wrongly considered to be morally good or bad, or rightly so. The Church has always held that circumstances have a great deal to do with the degree of responsibility for an action and the weight of its moral value and disvalue. But to believe that — aside from purely positive laws — what was considered a sin in the time of St. Augustine, St. Thomas, and St. Francis de Sales is no longer a sin today implies a clear contradiction of the teachings of Christ.

The Gospel is permeated with moral teachings

It is thus more than astonishing that Bishop Simons of Indore (India) should write an article that states that we now know that all morality refers exclusively to human welfare.[95] Certain things, therefore, hitherto considered immoral should no longer be so designated. He adds that, after all, apart from love of neighbor, Christ did not give any moral teaching in the Gospel.

Now, it is radically wrong and absolutely incompatible with Christian revelation to say that all morality has its source in the welfare of man. The core of morality is the glorification of God and the core of immorality is the offense against God. What was the

[95] *Cross Currents* 16 (1966): 429-45.

sin of Adam and Eve if not the tragic offense against God that separated humanity from Him? The thesis that man's welfare is the sole norm of morality smacks of utilitarianism and is completely erroneous, even from a purely philosophical point of view.

But it is hard to believe that a Bishop of the Holy Church could permit himself to declare that Christ did not give us specific moral teachings in the Gospel. Has he forgotten the Sermon on the Mount with its emphasis on the fundamental Christian virtues? Has he forgotten what Christ said to the young man who asked Him how he could reach perfection? Did not Christ reply by enumerating the commandments of the Decalogue? Is not the entire Gospel pervaded with an emphasis on moral goodness and the necessity of avoiding sin? What do we witness in the scene with Mary Magdalen? In the scene with the adulterous woman? Does not the glory of Christ's mercy presuppose the ultimate seriousness of their sinning?

Progressives seek to adapt religion to man

Even when Bishop Simons speaks about positive commandments, which by definition can change, the arguments he uses against the obligation of going to Mass on Sundays are very unfortunate. He says that since most men do not attend Mass anyway, this rule should be abolished.

In this assumption that the actual behavior of men should be the norm for suspending positive commandments of the Church, we again come upon the great secularizing error of our time: the idea that religion should be adapted to man, rather than man to religion.

22

False irenicism

A REACTION AGAINST the harshness of many of the condemnations of heretics in former centuries has provoked a growing antipathy to the very principle of condemning heresies. As is usually the case with simple reactions which have an emotional rather than a rational character, there is a failure to distinguish between the *abuse* and the *thing abused*. A man who has been several times disappointed may easily become a misanthropist. Similarly, as a reaction to a former harshness, a false irenicism is gaining currency among Catholics.

Charity requires that the Church condemn heresies

These persons seem unable to understand that the anathema pronounced by the infallible Church against all heresies is of the essence of Her mission and, moreover, is in no way incompatible with charity. Indeed, it is essentially connected with it.

We have already discussed the perversion of experiencing the essential exclusivity of truth as an infringement on one's freedom.

Here, a different aspect of this exclusivity is at issue — the protecting of truth from attack. Yet even some Catholics who experience the exclusivity of truth as liberating and who are not tempted to revolt against its alleged infringement on their freedom believe that the fight against error is uncharitable. The anathema of the Holy Church seems to them hard and inhuman. They have forgotten the admirable dictum of St. Augustine, "Kill the error; love the one who errs." They are unwilling to accept the idea that the killing of the error is inseparable from love for the one who errs. Their false irenicism makes them blind to the glorious character of the anathema when spoken by the infallible Church.

Anathemas protect the faith and the faithful

The protection of inalterable divine revelation necessarily requires the condemnation of all heresies. As predicted by Christ and the Apostles, heretics will try again and again to invade the Church. What would have become of Christian revelation had the Church not condemned Arianism, Pelagianism, Nestorianism, and Albigensianism? What would have happened if these heresies had been tolerated? What brought Cardinal Newman into the Church, although with a heavy heart for his dear Anglican friends, if not the insight that the Church had always defended truth against all heretics and that the doctrine of the Church had remained unspotted and gloriously unchanged, notwithstanding the doctrinal development toward ever greater explicitness?

The anathema against all errors that are essentially incompatible with Christ's revelation is not only a holy mission dictated by fidelity to Christ, but also an expression of the Church's holy love. The imperative call to repudiate error also flows out of Her holy love for all the members of the Mystical Body of Christ. The Church must protect them from being poisoned by error and thus alienated from Christ. The Church is also motivated by Her love for all those who are still outside Her fold and to whom the Church is charged to bring the light of Christ. The anathemas are the very test of the guidance of the Holy Spirit and the expression of the Church's loving protection of the faithful and Her charitable attempt to liberate and draw to Christ those possessed by error.

Charity calls us to correct others

It should not be forgotten that the words of St. Augustine apply not only to the anathema which is reserved exclusively to the infallible magisterium of the Church; they also imply that everyone should be eager to help liberate his neighbor from error, though with all due discretion. Too many have forgotten that real love can compel us to say "no" as well as "yes."

It is obvious that if a person tried to win us over to help him do something evil, we would have to refuse him — not only because of the offense to God which agreement to his proposal would involve, but also because charity would command us to do so. The sin that he intended to commit and for which he wanted our cooperation would also be a great evil to himself.

Charity calls us to teach others

But this "no" born of love is not restricted to the immoral proposals made to us by another. It extends also to the doctrinal errors in which another is ensnared. The effort to liberate him from error is a duty imposed by charity. Certainly it should not be done in a cool doctrinaire way that is tainted with pride. On the contrary and in every phase, the "killing of the error" should manifest in every phase an ardent love for him. In our fight against error we should be filled with a humble gratitude for the unmerited gift of having been granted the truth. Notwithstanding the fact that the immanent logic of "killing the error" can lead to an uncharitable attitude, that this attitude unfortunately has often been adopted, and that we must constantly guard against this danger, we are nevertheless required as a consequence of charity to persist in fighting error on behalf of truth.

When, out of a confused notion of charity, a soft-heartedness, or a superficial benevolence, we believe that we should leave the erring person in his error, we have ceased to take him seriously as a person and have no interest in his objective good.

Supernatural truths deserve a vigorous defense

False irenicism leaves us with the spectacle of persons who see the need for the propagation of truth, who accept the fight against wrong opinions in the field of natural truth — of science or philosophy — but who, when it comes to the active defense of divinely revealed truth, decide that the "killing of the error" is something hard and uncharitable. They fail to understand that errors concerning divine revelation call incomparably more for putting up a fight than do errors in the field of natural truth, because the consequences of the former errors are incomparably greater and even fatal.

Charity should permeate the killing of errors

As we noted, false irenicism is found not only among those who are unable or unwilling to see the threat to the Church in the secularism and apostasy that abounds in the ranks of the progressive Catholics. Many who see the danger within the Church believe that to unmask the dangers is somehow uncharitable. This is but one of the false reactions we discussed in Part I.

The fact that sometimes a great theologian's fight against heresy seemed to lack charity is no argument against the unmasking of heresies as such. We may take St. Augustine as our model, whose fight against Pelagianism was always permeated by charity for the heretic. People often insist rightly that the killing of the error does not guarantee charity toward the erring. But they do not as often remember the really decisive point: true charity absolutely requires the killing of the error.

Truth is more important than unity

False irenicism is motivated by a misconceived charity at the service of a meaningless unity.

It places unity above truth. Having severed the essential link between charity and defense of the truth, irenicism is more concerned with reaching a unity with all men than with leading them to Christ and His eternal truth. It ignores the fact that real unity can be reached only in truth. Our Lord's prayer "that they may be one"[96] implies being one in Him and must not be separated from His words in John: "And other sheep I have that are not of this fold. Them also I must bring and they shall hear my voice. And there shall be one fold and one shepherd."[97]

[96] John 17:11.

[97] John 10:16.

Part IV

Sacred and Secular

23

Dialogue

CONCERN ABOUT the isolation of the Church in the modern world played a great role in the Second Vatican Council and gave birth to an attempt to enter into a dialogue with other religions, as well as with the modern atheistic world.

The Church seeks to illumine other religions

This emphasis on dialogue means that the Church is no longer satisfied with merely rejecting atheistic errors or religions that are not illumined by the light of Christ.

Such rejection is one of the Church's most important missions and must remain fundamental and indispensable. But the Church is eager to detect all the true elements of other religions, to listen patiently to them, and to study ways in which the light of Christ might penetrate them. The Church also seeks to understand the causes of the grave disease of atheism and to discover what can be done to help remove the obstacles hindering atheists from finding their way to God.

Dialogue should not abandon truth

Dialogue means that one takes the other seriously and approaches him with reverence and love; but it in no way implies the alteration of divine revelation to suit the views of a partner in dialogue in order to come to an agreement more easily. Dialogue does not mean that so much as one iota of the essential doctrine of the Church can be changed or interpreted in such a way that a member of another religion or an atheist can "swallow" the doctrine of the Church without having to give up his former position.

Ecumenism should not compromise doctrine

The same must be said of ecumenism, which is something great and beautiful in its authentic meaning, but a dangerous slogan when interpreted as allowing or implying the possibility of doctrinal compromise.

Vatican II clearly warns against a misconceived ecumenism: "Nothing is more alien to ecumenism than this false irenicism, through which the purity of Catholic doctrine is jeopardized and its true and indubitable meaning obscured."[98]

Thus, when participating in dialogue we must never let ourselves be infected with the errors of others. Unfortunately, this is exactly what we see in those progressive Catholics who idolize the intellectual currents of the present epoch.

Their behavior recalls a letter I received many years ago from a Jesuit priest. It contained a loving and witty reference to one of his confreres who had been trying to reach young people infected with the National Socialist ideology by making compromises on the question of anti-Semitism. "My dear brother," he wrote, "has

[98] Decree on Ecumenism, *Unitatis Redintegratio*, Ch. 2, section 11.

interpreted St. Paul's counsel to 'weep with those who weep'[99] to mean: 'Become foolish with those who are foolish.' "

Abandonment of truth is not humility

Many of these Catholics consider themselves humble when they give up the claim that to the Church alone has been entrusted the fullness of divine revelation. But in reality, they only betray their lack of faith, their insecurity, and a combination of self-assertiveness and feelings of inferiority — all of which are far removed from humility. To be a relativist or a skeptic, to shrink from committing oneself unreservedly to truth, is certainly a typical outgrowth of pride. The acceptance of an evident natural truth is an indication of a certain humility, and the surrender of oneself to the absolute divine truth is the very soul of true humility.

True ecumenism presupposes a profound Catholic faith

For a Catholic, the indispensable prerequisite for a real and fruitful dialogue with the world is an absolute surrender to Christ and an unyielding adherence to the divine truth revealed by Him and expressed in the dogmas of the Holy Catholic Church. Those who lack this absolute faith and commitment should be firmly told that they are neither fit nor called upon to embark on a dialogue on behalf of the Church.

Dialogue is impossible with some atheists

In *Ecclesiam Suam*, Pope Paul clearly sets forth the different kinds of dialogue according to the degree of affinity one's partner's

[99] Rom. 12:15.

convictions have with Catholic doctrine. Obviously, the most important first question one must ask is whether one is engaged in a dialogue within the framework of ecumenism or whether one is talking with an atheist. This is not the place to analyze the ambiguity of the term *atheism* and to distinguish the varieties of atheism (each of which may call for a different approach). But there is one brand of atheism which we must discuss in some detail, for the question of dialogue with it has recently become a matter of some urgency.

It remains extremely doubtful that a real dialogue can be actualized between Catholics and atheistic Communists. We say a *real* dialogue because, unfortunately, alleged dialogues between Catholics and Communists are mushrooming everywhere, to the great confusion of the faithful.

As long as atheism is only a theoretical conviction, a dialogue with persons of this belief is possible. But when (as in National Socialism and Communism) atheism is a decisive element of a militant, highly organized party, especially of a party for which words have become weapons of propaganda, dialogue will lack its indispensable basis — namely, the shared assumption that the exchange of words constitutes a theoretical discussion.

If, for one of the participants, the dialogue is only another means of carrying on political warfare, there is no possibility for a genuine discussion. This is most emphatically the case in speaking with a member of a Communist Party or an agent of a Communist government. A dialogue with a Communist is possible only in the case of an individual person who may, theoretically, be a convinced Communist, but who is not actually either a representative of a Communist state or a member of the Communist Party.

It is surely obvious to everyone that a public declaration of sincerity is not at all sufficient to guarantee the genuineness of such a dialogue.

Because of the new popularity of such endeavors, it may be useful to pursue the theme of the danger of presuming that Catholics can really have a dialogue with Communists.

Equivocal language dooms fruitful dialogue

A disastrous habit of certain theologians popular among progressive Catholics is their equivocal use of terms. One crucial example is their use of the term *future*. One moment it refers to eternity; the next, to the historical future — that is, to the generations to come in the course of human history. But eternity and the historical future are such totally different realities that the term *future* cannot be used for both without falling into a complete equivocation. Teilhard de Chardin's naturalistic and evolutionalistic interpretation of man's destiny has obviously played a role in promoting this confusion.

Eternity concerns the individual

Eternity addresses itself to the individual person. It is the eternal life promised in the Gospel to the true followers of Christ and mentioned at the end of the Apostles' Creed. Eternal life transcends the empirically known world; its reality has been revealed to us.

The historical future concerns humanity

The historical future, on the contrary, is not at all a reference to an afterlife. It does not refer to the individual person at all; it is not *his* future. It refers to humanity, to coming generations. There is, of course, for every individual a natural future on earth — the future of "tomorrow." This is an essential dimension of time. Our life presents itself as a movement toward the future, the actualization of which we expect to experience. But this natural *personal* future clearly differs from the historical future to which evolutionalism and progressivism refer. The historical future in every earthly messianism,[100] for example, is clearly not limited to the lifetime of an individual person.

Eternity and the historical future are essentially different

This historical future lies in the field of the natural, empirically known world, and we can calculate many things about it with a degree of probability, even though we cannot really know how it will turn out or how far it will extend. But the essential thing to see is that the historical future is not an object of faith. It is not something supernatural; it does not transcend time, but unfolds specifically in time.

Eternity and the historical future thus differ so absolutely that it is not legitimate to treat them as if they were two species of the one genus "future." It will not suffice to call one the *absolute future* and the other the *non-absolute* (or simply the *future*). The only way to avoid equivocation and error is to confine the use of the term *future* to the historical reality.

Communism and Scripture relate to different "futures"

The abuse of language and the confusion of the faithful that are likely to emerge from these attempts to discuss religious questions with Marxists are exemplified in the "dialogue" that took place at Herrenchiemsee in September of 1966. Professor J. B. Metz and

[100]That is, belief in a coming Messiah.

Father Karl Rahner, S.J., asserted that the Gospel is above all concerned with the future. Now, this term can here refer only to men's eternal life, to those things that are the object of the theological virtue of hope. But then they immediately state that Marxism is also concerned with the future. And for Marxism the term can only refer to a merely historical, earthly future, a future that may be the expectation of a terrestrial messianism. The qualification that the Gospel is concerned with the "absolute future" fails to do justice to the radical difference between future as eternity and future as the merely historical to-come.

The ambiguity here is less an error than a deception. In fact, for the Communists eternity and eternal life are mere illusions or superstitions. For them *future* can only mean something that lies ahead for humanity in the coming centuries. It is not the future of an individual person, but of humanity — the human race.

Furthermore, it is quite misleading to say that the Gospel is basically concerned with this future. The message of Christ is primarily concerned with the sanctification and eternal salvation of the individual person. The historical future is brought up in the Gospel in the eschatological passages where the end of the world and Christ's second coming are predicted. But this eschatological future revealed in the Gospel cannot be separated from the eternity to which it is explicitly related. It loses all meaning if there is no eternity — no eternal life, no Heaven, and no Hell.

And when the Gospel speaks of the growth of the kingdom of God — as in the comparisons to the growth of the mustard seed in the parables — it is not the general historical future that is referred to. The entire emphasis is laid on the kingdom of God, the reality of the Mystical Body of Christ, and all the souls who will be saved and sanctified. The warnings to be found in the Gospel and St. Paul that evil times will come, that false Christs will arise, that the faithful will be tried, that many will apostatize, refer to the spiritual life of the Church and not to the natural course of history and the worldly conditions of humanity.

An emphasis on the historical future inevitably involves a collectivistic approach which is precluded by the absolutely personalistic nature of the Gospel, where every individual person is taken with ultimate seriousness. It is too often forgotten nowadays that the true community of which the doctrine of the Church speaks, the communion of the Mystical Body of Christ, the community of the militant, suffering, and triumphant Church, is essentially linked to the full appreciation of the individual person. It has nothing whatsoever to do with collectivism, which considers the individual as just a unit of the species, or as a mere part of the collective whole.

No desire for dialogue should blind us to the fact that concern for the future does not in the slightest define a community of interest between Marxists and Catholics.

The term *humanism* is used equivocally

A similar effort to generate an artificial basis for dialogue with Communists is to be seen in the equivocal use of the term *humanism*. There are undoubtedly several conceptions of humanism. We can speak of natural humanism — of the Greek ideal of humanism, for example, or of Goethe's. And it makes sense to say that Christian humanism differs from this merely natural humanism. When Maritain calls Christianity *the complete humanism* (*l'humanisme intégral*), he is quite rightly glancing at the incompleteness of the pagan ideal of humanism. One can also speak of an atheistic humanism, which Henri de Lubac treated in *The Drama of Atheist Humanism*. One might indeed call Nietzsche's ideal of the superman a humanism, or Feuerbach's ideal. But it makes no sense at all to speak of a Marxist or a Communist humanism.

Communism is incompatible with humanism

In the first place, the materialism of the Communist creed is incompatible with any ideal of humanism. If a man is nothing but some matter that has organized itself, then any talk of humanism can only be an equivocation. Certain features of man as a spiritual person are essential to every humanism. The humanistic ideal implies intellectual and moral values and their development. But the materialistic conception of man has no place for these values, even if, in practice, the Communist obviously cannot avoid taking intellectual values and achievements in some way into account.

In the second place, the idea of determinism according to the immanent laws of economic "science" (in historical materialism) is equally incompatible with a consistent humanism.

In the third place, the totalitarian nature of Communism, which takes the individual man as a means and measures his value strictly according to his usefulness to the collective, precludes any identification of Communism as a humanism. Communism is not surpassed by any ideology in its profound and consistent depersonalization. The person is deprived of every right.

We might just as well speak of the humanistic ideal of National Socialism where instead of the blunt materialism of Communism we find a biological materialism: racism. But it would obviously make no sense to consider National Socialism a type of humanism. Like Communism, it is a horrible anti-humanism, with a similar cult of depersonalization. Predictably enough, however, many of the very persons who would vehemently deny that National Socialism could ever be designated a form of humanism have no difficulty speaking of a Communist humanism, though the latter is every bit as hostile to true humanism as the former.

What has been said of the equivocal use of the term *future* applies equally to the equivocal use of the term *humanism*. To attempt to take an alleged common interest in humanism as a basis for dialogue — to conceive of Christianity and Communism as two varieties of humanism and then to say that the future will disclose which one is the more successful, more adequate to human needs — is to distort grotesquely the nature of dialogue and of humanism. Such a misrepresentation of the facts leads not to dialogue, but rather to a wishful (and dangerous) minimizing of the differences between Christianity and Communism.

Christian dialogue with Communists is dangerous

When Rahner wonders why the Communists do not accept a coexistence of the two attempts to reach the humanistic ideal, he betrays his blindness to the very essence of Communism. It is fully consistent for the Communists not to tolerate Christianity; for they are aware that what Christians call humanism has no place in Communist ideology and, in fact, forms a resolute obstacle to its plans.

The ambiguous use of terms by Catholics, therefore, only serves Communist propaganda and spreads confusion among Catholics themselves. This is not the kind of dialogue advocated by the Second Vatican Council.

24

Ecumenism and secularization

WHEN ONE READS what the Council has to say about ecumenism one is led to wonder how the progressive Catholics can manage explicitly to combine ecumenism and secularization. They desire to secularize the Church and at the same time they rave about a possible communion with religions outside the Church. Now, as the encyclical *Ecclesiam Suam* makes clear, there are several degrees of communion: first, with the Eastern, Byzantine Church; then, with the Protestants; then, with the Jews; then, with the Moslems; and, finally, with the Hindus and Buddhists. It is obviously incorrect to apply the term *ecumenism* to the dialogue with atheists.

Secularization undermines Christian ecumenism

True ecumenism implies that stress be laid on those elements which the Catholic Church possesses in common with other religions. Now it is well known that the Orthodox Church lays a special stress on the antagonism that exists between Christ and the spirit of "the world." She insists on the difference between the sacred and the profane. As a result, the Orthodox have often, though unjustly, accused the Catholic Church of making too many concessions to the profane, to the desacralized mentality of the modern occidental world. How can those who want to efface the signs of the incompatibility of the spirit of Christ and the spirit of the world, who want to desacralize the life of the Church, expect to attain a deeper communion with the Eastern Church?

The stress on the opposition between Christ and world is, on the one hand, something arch-Catholic and, on the other hand, precisely what the Eastern Church misses in Roman Catholicism. Is not the secularization advocated by the progressive Catholics the way to undermine any possibility of deeper relation and union with the Orthodox Churches?

A similar analysis leading to a similar conclusion can be applied to Lutheranism. In part, Luther's attacks on the Church were launched against Her worldliness. In his doctrine of the complete corrosion of nature through the fall of man, which leads to his thesis that man cannot be sanctified, there is implicit a special emphasis on eternity. Although his attitude toward nature is unbalanced, the primacy of God, of Christ the Redeemer, and of eternal life is still preserved.

Luther separates heaven and earth in a wrong way. In denying that moral values have a role to play in our salvation he abandons man to the sinful world; he thus secularizes man, but he does not secularize religion. He is far from believing that any attitude toward our neighbor (let alone toward "humanity") could ever replace our direct relation to, and our faith in, Christ. The words of many of Bach's cantatas testify to the absolute primacy Lutheranism accords heavenly things against all the things of this world.

Is it the purpose of ecumenism to foster communion with men of the evangelical faith of Luther, Melanchton, Bach, and Mathias

Claudius or communion with liberal Protestants like Robinson, Cox, or Fletcher who have lost their faith in Christ and have nothing in common with Protestants like Billy Graham who still believe? Obviously, ecumenism can only tend toward a communion with orthodox Protestants. And far from building a bridge, secularization actually places an obstacle between us and believing Protestants, for the primacy of heavenly things is certainly a positive factor in orthodox Protestantism, as is its aversion to the *saeculum*. Meetings with secularized Protestants cannot be considered a manifestation of true ecumenism, because in such cases the only possible common basis for discussion is secularization. That is, in matters of doctrine, we reach agreement with those who have lost their faith in Christ only by losing it ourselves (as Leslie Dewart's book, *The Future of Belief*, itself demonstrates).

Secularization hinders ecumenical relations with the Jews

As for the Jews, it should be apparent that an ecumenical spirit can only lead to communion with the Orthodox or possibly with the Conservative Jews — that is, with those who still believe in the Old Testament. Notwithstanding the deep dogmatic differences that separate Jews from Christians, their belief in the revelation of the Old Testament, their profound faith in God, their reverence, and their sense of the sacred constitute a powerful common basis.

Secularization harms relations with Eastern religions

Hinduism and Buddhism both contain a deep conviction of the irreality of the world — the *maya*. Unacceptable as this doctrine must be to Christians, the conviction that the fullness of reality lies beyond this world is nevertheless a valuable incomplete truth.

Though this transcendent reality is sought in a different direction, the metaphysical inferiority of the empirical world as compared with absolute reality is a common element which offers a basis for some communion. Common also is a stress on recollection and a sense of the difference between the sacred and the profane, for these are important in the oriental religions. It is not difficult to see that the secularization that certain Catholics would thrust on the Church undermines any possibility of ecumenical contact with Hinduism and Buddhism.

To be sure, secularization is an evil primarily because it implies an apostasy from Christ, and it is for this reason that we fight it on every page of this book. But it must also be emphasized that secularization stands in the way of true and authentic ecumenism.

25

Religious vitality and change

THE CAMPAIGN of the self-proclaimed avant-garde of the Church includes both the denigration of the Church's past and the heralding of change as a sign of vitality.

We have seen that *change* is an ambiguous and misleading term, for it may refer to two absolutely different phenomena: first, it may refer to a *radical alteration* — for example, the substitution of one ideal or conviction for another; and second, it may mean change in the sense of *growth* — the growth of our love, of our devotion, of our understanding. We have also seen that moral progress cannot consist in change in the first sense of the term.[101]

Spiritual progress presupposes continuity

For the Christian all progress consists in the second kind of change: in overcoming imperfections and cooperating more and

[101] See Chapter 12.

more in the process of sanctification that the Lord offers us in His teaching and in the sacraments. Striving for this is progress, indeed, and so essential is it for the Christian that Cardinal Newman says that if a man had attained a high degree of perfection and considered it sufficient, he would be worse off than a man who was a beginner on the road of perfection, yet filled with longing to be completely transformed in Christ.

Progress toward transformation in Christ necessarily implies continuity and perseverance: absolute fidelity to Christ, growing love for Christ, and growing horror for sin and false prophets. This stability and continuity is the very opposite of stagnation and complacency. Readiness to let oneself be changed and transformed by Christ is deeply interwoven with the continuity of an unchanging faith in Christ, for the progress at which the Christian aims implies a continual return to Christ from whom our fallen nature pulls us away.[102] Do not our lives show how we are menaced by infidelity, by slackening of fervor, by a steady drift to the periphery? In what can true progress consist if not in turning back to Christ?

Religious vitality involves a deepening of faith

It is a grave error to believe that vitality always implies change and that religion must undergo change if it is to remain alive. Certainly, while on this earth we are beings exposed to change. Our spiritual and bodily lives undergo change and development. But this change, rooted in our existence in time, does not mean that the objects of our convictions and loves also change. Truth — above all, supernatural truth — does not change, nor do values or their call for perseverance and steadfast adherence. In the very

[102] See Dietrich von Hildebrand, *Transformation in Christ* (Manchester, N.H.: Sophia Institute Press, 1990).

midst of change we can be stable in our deepest attitudes, in our fundamental convictions and our loves. In the realm of faith, aliveness means that our faith and our love never become mere habits, that we never cease to wonder, to delve anew into the unfathomable depth of revelation, which is the source of an ever-increasing religious vitality. Aliveness means that again and again we realize our full commitment to God.[103]

The nature of the change that takes place in our love and obedience to Christ as the fruits of the Holy Spirit bud forth in us is analogous to that indicated in the expression: "My love for you keeps growing in intensity and depth." It is the change proper to all growth in perfection; but it is obviously not the change about which the progressive Catholics are raving and which they erroneously consider to be the very essence of vitality.

Alteration of convictions is not religious vitality

Their conception of healthy change refers to altering our views and convictions, to replacing one love with another. This change implies discontinuity, unfaithfulness, and the complete absence of perseverance. Persons who frequently change their convictions, going from one false prophet to another, do not exhibit a plenitude of life. Rather, their oscillations are only a semblance of vitality. In this state, nothing can take root in their souls and everything in them will be stillborn. To consider this kind of change an indication of spiritual aliveness is an error similar to taking pluralism in philosophy or religion for a sign of intellectual vitality.

[103]The confusion about change and religion that characterizes the thinking of progressive Catholics reached an extreme of absurdity in the following remark of a priest: "Change . . . is the most stable quality in the Church" (*Triumph*, 1, No. 4 [December 1966]: 34).

Conversion is radical change rather than progress

When a profound conversion does occur in a person's spiritual life, it cannot be said to take place *within* the framework of his religious life; rather, this *metanoia* precedes, or is the very beginning of, his religious life. The term *progress* or *growth* would be quite inadequate to describe this critical phenomenon.

The radical change in religious conversion is a mark of vitality, not because it is a change, but because it is a turning from error to divine truth, a transition from death to life. St. Augustine had this in mind when he said of the struggles preceding his conversion: "I still hesitated to live unto life and die unto death."[104]

Radical change does not occur in a vital faith

We have time and again stressed the absolute character of divinely revealed truth. But it cannot be said too often that neither in the religious life of the individual nor in the doctrine of the Church is there any place for radical change. There are those who say, "We no longer want to hear of the passion of Christ and of His resurrection; we no longer want to strive for holiness; what we must be given are *new* ideas, *new* views, *new* goals; otherwise, our religious life will dry out." Those who say this are betraying unmistakably that their faith is dead.

They cannot understand that the mysteries of faith are inexhaustible and unfathomable. To speak of change or progress in the Church can mean the growth of the Kingdom of God in the souls of men, the growth in holiness of all members of the Mystical Body of Christ. It can mean the growth in explicitness of formulation of

[104] *Confessions*, Bk. 8, Ch. 11.

the divine revelation entrusted to the Church. But it can never mean any change in the sense of the substitution of a new content of belief or a new dogma for an old one.

The Church in Her faith remains ever the same

It is an essential mark of the true Church that unlike all purely human institutions and communities, She remains forever one and the same in the faith She guards. The identity of the Church of the Catacombs with the Church of the Nicene Council, of the Church of the Tridentine Council with the Church of the Vatican Councils is a sign that She is a divine institution. A Church of "tomorrow" that would replace a Church of "yesterday" would be a contradiction of the very nature of the Church. He whose heart is more thrilled by the idea of a changing Church than by the glorious identity and stability of the Church has lost the *sensus supranaturalis* and shows that he no longer loves the Church.

Renewal in the Church eliminates infidelities

As we have indicated in Part I, changes productive of renewal and vivification in the Church are concerned essentially with elimination of the infidelities that invade the sanctuary of the Church. Renewal, therefore, involves in the first instance a continual return to the one unchanging call of the Lord, to the authentic, pure, and unchanging goal of holiness. It is the very opposite of the changing rhythm of history.

Growth in holiness is true progress for the Church

No doubt, there are many things on the periphery of Church life that do change according to historical conditions. But the taking into account of a given historical situation can affect only positive prescriptions. Certain religious customs well adapted to one epoch may call for a change in another. The reduction of fasting in modern times, for example, is certainly something necessary because of the reduced vitality and the nervous strain of modern life. But it would be wrong to call this change a *progress*, for the change does not amount to the elimination of a disvalue or the replacement of a lesser value by a higher value.

But when Pius X encouraged daily Communion, he was reviving a practice that was widespread in early Christian centuries and, to the extent that it has been adopted, it means a progress, an increase in perfection in the lives of the faithful. Likewise, a change in canon law designed to correct certain abuses may be a progress in the life of the Church.

The existence of the Church is a sign of religious vitality

In our discussion (in Chapter 11) of the socio-historical reality of ideas, we saw that the vitality of ideas that are in the air in a given epoch has a special character when these ideas are true and when they refer to something having a definite value. In this case, the socio-historical reality takes on the nature of a fulfillment, because the true and the good ought to be professed and adhered to. Truth is meant to reign among men; the victory of truth and value is the fulfillment of an oughtness. Compared with the reality and vitality that the reign of true ideas or the triumph of good possesses, the historical reality of errors is only a sham aliveness.

But the historical reality of the Church has an incomparable significance. Quite apart from the extent of its acceptance among men, the very fact of the existence of the Church is a victory for Christ. The Church represents a unique socio-historical reality in the fact that the visible Church pours a stream of grace into the souls of men through the sacraments, that She is guided by the Holy Spirit, and that in the midst of the world She announces unspotted divine revelation to mankind, the message of divine mercy.

That the Church summons men to conversion and exhorts them to strive for holiness is in itself a unique actualization of the Kingdom of Christ. The fact that human beings are humbly confessing their sins and that the word of God is being proclaimed *opportune, importune* is a unique triumph of the spirit of Christ. The very existence of the uninterrupted apostolic succession of the papacy and of the many religious orders testifies to the incontestable victory of Christ over the world. And in view of the host of saints in the two thousand years of Christianity, each of whom represents an irruption of the supernatural into this world, who could deny that the words on the obelisk before St. Peter's Basilica have achieved full reality: *Christus vincit, Christus regnat, Christus imperat* (Christ conquers, Christ reigns, Christ rules)?

We must ever pray "Thy kingdom come"

Although the very existence of the Church is a sign of a unique and luminous vitality independent of the fortunes of the Church in the world, there is an indefinite range of realizations of the Kingdom of God yet to come. Thus, the faithful continue to pray daily, "Thy kingdom come." Innumerable men are still sitting in the shadow of death.[105] Innumerable members of the Mystical Body are not yet transformed in Christ. Time and again, as Cardinal Newman says, Christ draws us, tepid and unfaithful servants, into His Church "by cords of Adam":

[105]Ps. 22:4 (RSV = Ps. 23:4).

> And what are those cords? . . . It is the manifestation of the glory of God in the face of Jesus Christ; it is that view of the attributes and perfections of Almighty God; it is the beauty of His sanctity, the sweetness of His mercy, the brightness of His heaven, the majesty of His law, the harmony of His providences, the thrilling music of His voice, which is the antagonist of the flesh, and the soul's champion against the world and the devil.[106]

[106]John Henry Cardinal Newman, *Discourses Addressed to Mixed Congregations* (London: Longmans, 1916), 69.

26

The role of beauty in religion

BEAUTY PLAYS an important role in religious worship. The very act of worshipping a divinity implies a desire to surround the cult dedicated to this divinity with beauty. To stigmatize as *aestheticism* the concern for beauty in the religious cult (as some Catholics are doing lately with increasing stridency) betrays a distorted conception of religious worship as well as of the nature of beauty. This becomes clear when one considers the nature of aestheticism instead of merely employing the term as a destructive slogan.

Aestheticism is a perverse approach to beauty

Aestheticism is a perversion of the approach to beauty. The aesthete enjoys beautiful things as one enjoys good wine. He does not approach them with reverence and with an understanding of the intrinsic value calling for an adequate response, but as sources of subjective satisfaction merely. Even if he has a refined taste and is a remarkable connoisseur, the aesthete's approach cannot possibly do justice to the nature of beauty.

Above all, he is indifferent to all the other values that may inhere in the object. Whatever the theme of a situation may be, he looks at it solely from the point of view of his aesthetic enjoyment or pleasure. His fault does not lie in overrating the value of beauty, but in ignoring the other fundamental values — above all, moral values.

Goods must be appreciated in conformity with their value

To approach a situation from a point of view that does not correspond to its objective theme is always a great perversion. For example, it is perverse for a man to approach a human drama that calls for compassion, sympathy, and helpful action as if it were merely an object for psychological study. To make scientific analysis the only point of view in every approach is radically unobjective and even repulsive; it disregards and nullifies the objective theme. Apart from ignoring all other points of view than the "aesthetic" and all other themes than that of beauty, the aesthete also distorts the real nature of beauty in its depth and grandeur. As we have shown in other books, all idolization of a good necessarily precludes understanding its true value. The greatest, the most authentic appreciation of a good is possible only if we see it in its objective place in the God-given hierarchy of being.

Reverence should increase love of beauty

If someone were to refuse to go to Mass because the church was ugly or the music mediocre, he would be guilty of aestheticism, for he would have substituted the aesthetic point of view for the religious one. But it is the antithesis of aestheticism to appreciate the great function of beauty in religion, to understand both the legitimate role it should play in the cult and the desire of religious men to invest the greatest beauty in all things pertaining to the worship of God. This correct appreciation of beauty is rather an organic outgrowth of reverence, of love of Christ, of the very act of adoration.

Beauty is not opposed to evangelical poverty

Unfortunately, some Catholics claim today that this desire to endow the cult with beauty is in opposition to evangelical poverty. This grave error seems often to be bolstered by feelings of guilt for having been indifferent to social injustices and for having neglected the legitimate claims of the poor. In the name of evangelical poverty, then, we are told that the churches should be bare, simple, and deprived of all unnecessary adornments.

The Catholics who suggest this are confusing evangelical poverty with the prosaic, humdrum character of our modern world. They have lost sight of the fact that the replacement of beauty by comfort, and the luxury this often entails, is much more antithetical to evangelical poverty than beauty, even in its most exuberant forms, could ever be. The functionalist notion of what is superfluous is very ambiguous, a mere outgrowth of utilitarianism. It contradicts the words of our Lord: "Men do not live by bread alone."[107]

In *The New Tower of Babel*, we have tried to show that all culture is a superabundant gift, something that must seem superfluous to the utilitarian mind. But, thank God, the latter was not the attitude of the Church and the faithful through the centuries. St. Francis, who in his own life practiced evangelical poverty in the extreme, never claimed that the churches should be dry, bare, and without beauty. On the contrary, the church and its altar

[107]Matt. 4:4; Luke 4:4.

could never be beautiful enough for him. The same can be said of the Curé of Ars, St. John Vianney.

Luxury is in conflict with evangelical poverty

A ridiculous paradox is produced when, on behalf of evangelical poverty, the artistically most precious churches are torn down and replaced — at great cost — with prosaic and bare churches.[108] It is not the beauty and splendor of the church, the house of God, that is incompatible with the spirit of evangelical poverty and gives scandal to the poor, but rather the unnecessary luxury and comfort so widespread today. If the clergy want to return to evangelical poverty, they should recognize that in countries like the United States and Germany the clergy possess the most elegant cars, the best cameras, the most up-to-date television sets. Much drinking and smoking is definitely opposed to evangelical poverty, but certainly not the beauty and splendor of the churches.

On the one hand, it is claimed that churches should be bare; but on the other hand, in parishes and on the campuses of Catholic colleges, ugly buildings for social affairs, endowed with every kind of unnecessary luxury, are built; and this is done in the name of social concern and community spirit. Even in convents, one finds analogous developments. These new structures are not only opposed to evangelical poverty; they exhale a specifically worldly atmosphere. The reclining chairs and thick carpets have an unhealthy softness. These buildings artfully combine three negative qualities: expensiveness (which is directly opposed to evangelical poverty), ugliness, and an invitation to the self-indulgence that typifies the degeneracy menacing man in our times.

[108] For examples, see Michel de Saint Pierre, *Sainte Colère* (Paris: Editions de La Table Ronde, 1965), 175.

The Liturgy should create a sacred atmosphere

Sometimes the arguments for iconoclasm take another turn. One can occasionally hear pastors claim that the Holy Mass is something abstract and that the churches, and especially the altar, should therefore be bare. In reality, Holy Mass is an incredible mystery, transcending all our rational understanding; but in no way is it anything abstract.

The abstract is specifically rational and is opposed to the real, the concrete, the individual. The world of the supernatural, the reality that has been revealed, transcends the world of the rational, but this implies no contrast to the real or concrete. It is, on the contrary, the ultimate, absolute, although invisible, reality. The Mass, then, is the epitome of concrete reality, for Christ Himself is truly present.

The power and existential impact of the sacred Liturgy is precisely rooted in the fact that it is in no way abstract and addresses itself not only to our intellect or a naked faith, but rather speaks to the entire human person in innumerable ways. It immerses the faithful in the sacred atmosphere of Christ through the sacred beauty and splendor of the churches, through the color and beauty of the vestments, through the style of its language and the sublime music of the Gregorian chant.

The form of the Liturgy should reflect its importance

Sometimes progressive Catholics claim that those who fight against modern iconoclasm are concerned with the "unessential."

It is indeed not essential that the church in which Holy Mass is celebrated and in which the faithful receive Holy Communion be beautiful. Only the words through which transubstantiation is accomplished are essential. If this is what is referred to, then one can have no objection. But if by *unessential* is meant "insignificant," if it is meant that such things as the beauty of the church, the Liturgy, and the music are trivial, then this accusation is very wrong, for there is a profound relation between the essence of something and its adequate expression. This is especially true of Holy Mass.

The way in which this mystery is presented, its visible appearance, plays a definite role and cannot be considered subject to arbitrary change despite the fact that the thing expressed is incomparably more important than its expression. Although the real theme of the Mass is the making present of the mystery of Christ's sacrifice on the Cross and the mystery of the Eucharist, a great weight should nevertheless be put on the sacred atmosphere generated by the words, the activities, the accompanying music, and the church in which it takes place. None of these things can be considered to have a merely aesthetic interest.

In contradistinction to all gnostic denigration of matter and external expression is the specifically Christian principle that spiritual attitudes should also find their adequate expression in the demeanor of our body and our movements and in the style of our words. All the Liturgy is pervaded by this principle. Analogously, the room or building in which solemn and sacred things take place should emanate an atmosphere which corresponds to them. To be sure, the reality of these mysteries is not affected if their expression is inadequate. But there is a specific value in their being given adequate expression.

Beauty lifts our souls to God

How wrong it is, therefore, to consider the beauty of the church and of the Liturgy as something that might distract us and draw us away from the real theme of the liturgical mysteries to something superficial! Those who clamor that the church is no museum and that the really pious man is indifferent to these accidentals only show their blindness to the great role played by adequate (and beautiful) expression. Ultimately, this is a blindness to man's nature. Although they claim to be "existential," these persons remain very abstract. They forget that authentic beauty contains a specific message of God which lifts up our souls. As Plato said: "At the sight of beauty, our souls grow wings."[109]

Moreover, the sacred beauty connected with the Liturgy never claims to be thematic, as in a work of art; rather, as expression, it has a serving function. Far from obscuring or replacing the religious theme of the Liturgy, it helps it to shine forth.

Beauty has value even when it is not essential

Value is not synonymous with indispensability. The basic principle of superabundance in all creation and in all culture manifests itself precisely in values that are not indispensable for a certain end or theme. The beauty of nature is not indispensable to the household of nature. Nor is the beauty of architecture indispensable to our lives. But the value of beauty in nature and in architecture is not diminished by the fact that it is a pure gift, superabundantly transcending mere utility.

Thus, beauty has an importance not only when it is the theme (as in a work of art), but also when it has a purely serving function for another theme. To stress that the Liturgy should be beautiful in no way amounts to the coloring of religion with an aesthetic approach. The longing for beauty in the Liturgy simply arises from the sense of the specific value which lies in the adequacy of expression.

[109] *Phaedrus* 249d.

Sacred beauty promotes our sanctification

The beauty and sacred atmosphere of the Liturgy are not only something precious and valuable as such (as adequate expressions of the religious acts of worship), but are also of great importance for the development of the souls of the faithful. Time and again those in the liturgical movement have stressed the truth that mawkish prayers and hymns distort the religious ethos of the faithful; appealing to centers in man that are far removed from the religious one, they draw him into an atmosphere which obscures and blurs the face of Christ. Sacred beauty, therefore, is of great importance for the formation of the true ethos of the faithful.

In *Liturgy and Personality*[110] I consider in detail the profound function the Liturgy has for our sanctification, despite the fact that the worship of God is rather the theme of the Liturgy. In the Liturgy we praise and thank God; we partake in Christ's sacrifice and prayer. By inviting us to pray with Christ to God, the Liturgy also plays a fundamental role in our transformation in Christ. This role is not restricted to the supernatural part of the Liturgy. It also pertains to its form, to the sacred beauty embodied in the words and music of the Holy Mass or the Divine Office. To overlook this fact is a sign of great primitiveness, mediocrity, and lack of realism.

Worldly art or music has no place in the Mass

One of the great aims of the liturgical movement has been to replace unsuitable prayers and hymns with the sacred text of the official liturgical prayers and by the Gregorian chant. Today, however, we are witnessing a crippling of this liturgical movement as many try to replace the sublime Latin text of the Liturgy with

[110]Manchester, N.H.: Sophia Institute Press, 1993.

translations into vernacular slang. They even arbitrarily change the Liturgy itself in order to "adapt it to our time." Gregorian chant is replaced at best by mediocre music, at worst by jazz or rock and roll. Such grotesque substitutions veil the spirit of Christ immeasurably more than did former sentimental types of devotion.

Those were certainly inadequate. However, jazz is not only inadequate, but antithetical to the sacred atmosphere of the Liturgy. It is more than a distortion; it also draws men into a specifically worldly atmosphere. It appeals to something in men that makes them deaf to the message of Christ.

Churches should have a sacred atmosphere

Even when sacred beauty is replaced, not by profane vulgarity, but by neutral abstractions, this has serious consequences for the lives of the faithful. For, as we have indicated, the Catholic Liturgy excels in its appeal to a man's entire personality. The faithful are not drawn into the world of Christ only by their faith or by strict symbols. They are also drawn into a higher world by the beauty of the church, its sacred atmosphere, the splendor of the altar, the rhythm of the liturgical texts, and by the sublimity of the Gregorian chant or other truly sacred music — for example, a mass by Mozart or by Bach. Even the odor of incense has a meaningful function to perform in this direction. The use of all channels capable of introducing us into the sanctuary is deeply realistic and deeply Catholic. It is truly existential and plays a great role in helping us lift up our hearts.

The Second Vatican Council favored the Latin Mass

While it is true that pastoral considerations may make use of the vernacular desirable, the Latin Mass (whether as silent Mass, dialogue Mass, or especially as sung Mass with Gregorian chant — should never be abandoned. It is not a question of granting the Latin Mass a place for a certain time until all the faithful are accustomed to the vernacular Mass. As the Vatican Council's Constitution on the Sacred Liturgy clearly states, the vernacular is permitted, but the Latin Mass and the Gregorian chant retain their full importance.[111]

That was the intention of the *motu proprio*[112] of St. Pius X which stated that the unique sacred atmosphere of the diction of the Latin Mass, as well as that of the Gregorian chant, should form the piety of the faithful. Thus, the demands of many Catholics and the *Una Voce* movements are not directed against the use of the vernacular, but against the growing elimination of the Latin Mass and the Gregorian chant. They are simply asking that the Constitution on the Liturgy really be followed.[113]

The Liturgy must never be secularized

Yet certain Catholics today express the desire of changing the external form of the Liturgy by adapting it to the style of life of our desacralized age. Such a desire indicates a blindness to the nature of the Liturgy, as well as a lack of reverence and gratitude for the sublime gifts of two thousand years of Christian life. It betrays a ludicrous self-assurance and conceit to believe that these traditional forms can be scrapped for something better. And this conceit is especially incongruous in those who accuse the Church of

[111] *Sacrosanctum concilium*, Ch. 3, "The Reform of the Sacred Liturgy," section 36, paragraphs 1-4.

[112] A rescript issued by the Pope on matters initiated by himself.

[113] See my article "The Case for the Latin Mass," *Triumph*, 1, No. 2 (October 1966).

"triumphalism." On the one hand, they consider a lack of humility the Church's claim that She alone possesses the full divine revelation (instead of perceiving that this claim is rooted in the very nature of the Church and flows out of Her divine mission). On the other hand, they exhibit a ridiculous pride in assuming that our modern epoch is superior to former ones.[114]

[114]Today we can hear voices protesting, for example, that the wording of the *Gloria* and of other parts of the Mass is filled with boring expressions praising and glorifying God, when it should be referring to our daily lives. See, for example, the argument for a "relevant" translation of the Mass in Gareth Edwards' article on modern English in the Mass in *America* 115 (1966): 483-86. Such nonsense discloses again how right Lichtenberg was when he said that if an ape were to read St. Paul's epistles, he would see his own image reflected in them. One wonders if our modern theologians will not soon present us with a new version of the *Our Father*, as Hitler did. The *Our Father* obviously emphasizes the absolute primacy of God that is so alien to a typical modern mentality. Only one petition ("Give us this day our daily bread") refers to man's earthly welfare. The rest of the prayer is concerned with God, His Kingdom, and our eternal welfare.

27

The word of the Lord

CERTAIN EXPERTS in modern scriptural exegesis claim that Christ's words as related in the Gospels must be taken as authentic in their meaning only, not in their wording. While we prescind here from the question of whether or not this theory is true, we must remark that many of the proposals that were boldly put forward by liberal Protestant exegetes soon ceased to be taken seriously. But the question arises: Should the received wording of the Gospels be replaced by any other?

The assumption of those who answer the question affirmatively is that because Christ spoke to the people of His epoch in language they understood, the Church should retranslate His message into the language of each succeeding epoch. This assumption rests on an equivocation. As long as it refers to homilies, it is correct. It is indeed evident that a reference to the contemporary period is called for in a homily although, besides being timely, the wording should always be simple and suggestive of the sacred. But when this assumption is applied to the sayings of Christ, it is most incorrect.

Christ's words have power, simplicity, and sacredness

Any change in the words of Christ as received would be a calamitous mistake. They have a unique flavor: they are not only evocative of the sacred, but have a mysterious, inexhaustible fertility and power. Simplicity and concreteness are bathed by a timeless divine atmosphere. They have touched countless souls through two thousand years, from the simplest and naive to the greatest geniuses. These words have changed human lives and opened to them the way of salvation. The ring of Christ's words as we know them is absolutely irreplaceable.

Is it only accidental that Jesus was born in Bethlehem in Palestine at a certain moment in history? Does not the choice of time and place also belong to the revelation? And should not the evangelical wording of Christ's message, born from the sacred living tradition of the young Church, be accepted with the greatest reverence? Have not these words been the salt of the entire Liturgy and the fecundating power in the lives and thoughts of the Fathers and Doctors of the Church? What would have become of the Church if in every generation new wording had been adopted in the style dominant at the moment — a rationalist style in the eighteenth century, a romantic one at the beginning of the nineteenth century, and so on?

His exact words should echo through all times and places

Does it not belong to the very nature of divine revelation that the wording of Christ's message should resound through all the centuries in its unparalleled beauty, its timeless and always timely sacred atmosphere, and its never diminishing power? Does it not belong to the nature of divine revelation that these words should achieve an independence of all styles and fashions, all expression peculiar to a given time, all slang and jargon? Has not the history of two thousand years manifested an inexhaustible plenitude, not only in the meaning, but also in the unique style of the sacred writings? Has not their expression been reverently preserved by all Protestants, not to mention the Orthodox Church? Does it not belong to the nature of Christ's message that in its wording as well as its meaning it should draw man out of the changing atmosphere of the *saeculum* into the sacred world, the world of God?

It is a fundamental error to believe that the divine message should be offered in profane, worldly vessels so it might become a more organic part of the lives of the faithful. On the contrary, the entire Liturgy was built on the principle that the mysteries of worship should be offered in vessels emanating an atmosphere corresponding, as far as possible, to the sacredness of their content.

Worldly translations undermine faith in Christ

In spite of this, there is a tendency today to translate the New Testament into a humdrum and almost slang vernacular with the purpose of bringing it closer to the people. But this, we repeat, is a grave mistake. It forgets that if Christ is fully man, His humanity as God-man is a sacred one; it emanates an indescribable holiness. The holiness of Christ's Sacred Humanity is the very basis of our faith. It was the epiphany of God in Jesus that overwhelmed the Apostles and made them follow Him, "having left all things behind them."[115] It is the Sacred Humanity of Christ, beyond all possible ideals fabricated by a human mind, that compels us to adore Him as God-man.

To present the words of Christ in a trivial, everyday manner is a way of undermining the image of Christ in the faithful and of

[115]Luke 5:11; Mark 10:28; Matt. 19:27.

jeopardizing their faith in the process. If all the prophets speak to us in a solemn manner, if the epistles of Peter, Paul, and John convey Christian revelation in a sublime and solemn way, what fantastic logic can have led persons to translate an *Amen, dico vobis* ("Amen, I say unto you") as "Let me tell you," when the text following is of such an ultimate, prophetic import as "Heaven and earth shall pass away, but my words shall not pass away."[116] This stripping from the words of all solemnity and grandeur, of something that is always associated with religious texts — especially with the words of the prophets of the Old Covenant and above all with the message of the God-man Christ — is done in the name of bringing Christ's message closer to the faithful. But this psychologically awkward and primitive move in reality screens and even falsifies the image of Christ, and thereby only serves to undermine faith in His message.

[116]Mark 13:31; Luke 21:33.

28

Tradition

WE HAVE ALREADY DISCUSSED the disastrous dethronement of truth and value that historical relativism entails. We have also emphasized that this spiritual disease has spread rather widely among progressive Catholics. We now wish to take up the paradoxical fact that historical relativism strips history of its nature and meaning.

On the one hand, the proponents of historical relativism wish to make of history the ultimate measure of all things; they wish to absolutize history. It has, for example, become fashionable among progressive Catholics to speak of man's "responsibilities to history." (Our responsibilities to God are somehow relegated to the background.)

But on the other hand, the dethronement of truth and the debunking of all objective values has the consequence of destroying tradition. And this is to deny any meaning to history.

To kill tradition brings about the dissolution of history, for history presupposes tradition. The analogy that has often been drawn between the life of an individual person and the history of humanity may help shed light on the essential and indispensable role tradition plays in history. If a man did not possess the capacity of conserving the past and was nourished exclusively by the present moment, if his life lacked all continuity, he would no longer be a person. A history of his own life would be impossible. There is no history of dogs or cats. There can only be a history of persons.

Tradition preserves timeless values

In the history of mankind, tradition has a function analogous to that of continuity in the life of an individual person. Furthermore, continuity in the life of the individual assumes its profound significance only through the fact that there are great truths and high values which, when disclosed to him, call for a perseverant clinging to them. Analogously, if there is no objective value except that of being "up-to-date," it follows that tradition, the transmission of truth, of ideals, of cultural treasures, is meaningless and there can be no meaning in history. Kierkegaard expressed this point as follows: "If the moment is everything, the moment is nothing."

Significant history implies that there is a tradition of insights and works of art that are timeless, that are beyond time in their importance, validity, and value. The significance of tradition resides in the fact that there are things which, because of their intrinsic value and their truth, have a message for man in every epoch. These are things that can never be superannuated.

No valid and fruitful tradition could ever exist independently of timeless contributions such as those made by Plato, Aristotle, St. Augustine, Dante, Shakespeare, Michelangelo, Bach, and, of course, Beethoven. They are always timely on account of their timelessness, for to be timeless is not to be unrelated to time, but rather, to be valid at all times.

Debunkers of tradition often know little about history

Yet progressive Catholics who declare, "We have loved the past too long," not only undermine the very meaning of history in their assault on tradition; they also often exhibit a deplorable ignorance in historical matters. They shift man's responsibility from God to history. But if responsibility to history has any meaning, they fail to live up to their "obligations" either by making dilettante judgments about historical facts or by misinterpreting history in order to lend credibility to their prejudices.

History shows the Church to be a font of charity

For example, there is a fashionable argument which runs as follows: Christians in past centuries lacked charity for men and showed love only for God, whereas atheists, while rejecting God, have loved men.[117] It is difficult to say whether this assertion is remarkable more for the ignorance of history it betrays or for the ambiguity of its use of the terms *atheist* and *Christian*. Anyone who knows anything about the two thousand years of Christian history is familiar with the fact that the love of Christ blossomed forth in a unique love for the poor, the suffering, and the sick — in a sublime charity that expressed itself in forgiveness for one's enemies.

Have these "modern" Catholics who have made history their God never read a biography of St. Francis of Assisi, of St. John of God, or of St. Vincent de Paul? Have they never heard about the heroic sacrifices of missionaries who did not preoccupy themselves exclusively with the salvation of the souls of pagans, but also fed

[117]Cf. the example in William Fitzpatrick's article on the Oklahoma diocese, *Triumph*, 1, No. 4 (December 1966).

the hungry and cared for the sick (though the former was a sign of a much deeper interest in their fellow men than any concern for their physical welfare could have been)? Have these Catholics who are so eager to attack the record of the Church never heard of the fact that hospitals were "invented" by religious and for centuries administered exclusively by them? Have they never heard that even the *mont de piété*[118] was invented by the religious, or that the order of the Trinitarians was founded to liberate Christians imprisoned by Moslems?

Anyone who studies the history of the Church without prejudging it cannot but acknowledge that from all those who really lived Christianity there flowed an ardent and sublime love for their neighbor, and even for their enemies and persecutors. Their love was of the essence of holiness, of their transformation in Christ. It has always been at the core of the teaching of the Church. This charity was something completely new, unknown to the pagan world; and it was *this* charity that converted countless pagans.

That charity for their neighbor was lacking in many Christians, nobody can deny. But was it because they loved God instead, or because they were bad Christians and did not love God enough, were not transformed in Christ — were, in fact, mediocre Christians? Two thousand years of Christian history produced a great stream of charity and heroic deeds of love for men. And history shows that this charity was to be found in proportion to men's love of God, to their devotion to Christ. Since the majority of Christians have always been tepid in their love of God and failed to live up to the teachings of Christ, their love for their neighbor has suffered from the same imperfection.

[118] A type of pawn-shop, where one could receive a loan of money in exchange for some article, run on a non-profit basis by the Church in Paris.

Atheism does not lead to charity

The other half of the argument, which asserts that atheists have excelled in their love for men, also needs proof. The National Socialists yesterday and the Communists today are the most radical atheists and perhaps the most radical haters of Christ who have ever existed. It would be difficult indeed to see a testament of love for men in the murder of six or seven million people by the German National Socialists or in the Communists' murder of several times that number. Are concentration camps and the abolition of all personal rights the marks of a special love for men?

We certainly do not mean that every type of atheism necessarily produces such atrocities. History shows that many atheists have had a benevolent interest in their fellow men. But it is by no means sure that this benevolent interest (which, incidentally, differs radically from Christian charity) stems from their atheism.

To claim that the modern concern for social justice is the outgrowth of atheism because many of the champions of humanitarian movements have been atheists ignores the fact that many faithful Catholics, Protestants, and Jews have also participated in these movements. The increased efficiency and effectiveness that modern science and technology make possible can hardly be considered symptoms of greater love for man. The institutional nature of modern charitable organizations, which tends to kill the intimate personal devotion to one's neighbor that was typical of former times, is clearly not a sign of the superior charity of the contemporary world.

Charity differs essentially from humanitarian benevolence

But the most important thing for our purpose is the radical difference between the humanitarian benevolence of atheists and the sublime Christian charity of which St. Paul speaks. He who has eyes to see and ears to hear cannot but grasp the difference between the attitude of a St. Francis embracing the leper and the humanitarian zeal of certain contemporary atheists.

Many progressive Catholics believe that by stressing the black side of the history of the Church — that is, the failure of many to live up to the call of Christ — they are being very objective and humble; after all, they are accusing their own Church. But in fact, this attitude is not at all the humble *mea culpa* (*my* fault) of the *Confiteor*, but an arrogant *vestra culpa* (*your* fault). For these Catholics have given up their solidarity with the Church of yesterday. Consequently, their condemnation of the past under the guise of self-accusation is pharisaical.

The Church remains spotless even when Her members sin

We do not deny that the human history of the Church, like all human history, has its black pages. We simply urge that if one wishes to take an objective look at history, one must acknowledge that the doctrine of the Church has always implicitly condemned abuses introduced by Her members. There were sinners in the Church yesterday and there are sinners in the Church today. But the Church Herself, in Her divine teaching, emerges gloriously unspotted in a history stained by human weaknesses, errors, imperfections, and sins.[119] The miracle of the host of saints She has

[119]Maritain quotes Cardinal Journet as follows: "All contradictions are eliminated as soon as we understand that the members of the Church do indeed sin, but they do so by their betraying the Church. The Church is thus not without sinners, but She is without sin.

"The Church as person is responsible for penance. She is not responsible for sins. . . . The members of the Church themselves — laity, clerics, priests, bishops, and Popes — who disobey the Church are responsible for

produced in the course of Her history distinguishes Her history from all other human institutions and testifies to Her divinity.

The Church's tradition differs from other traditions

We have dealt extensively with the nature of tradition in *Graven Images: Substitutes for True Morality.*[120] There we stress the radical difference between the Church's tradition based on divine revelation and all merely human traditions. The revelation of the Old Testament and the self-revelation of God in Christ are the unique source of the divine truth that has been entrusted to the Church by God. The unique nature of this supernatural tradition manifests itself in the fact that identity with the divine revelation entrusted to the Apostles is the all-important, though not the exclusive, argument for the truth of any dogma.

The Church's cultural tradition reflects Her holy life

Even the historical, cultural tradition of the Church, notwithstanding its radical difference from the supernatural, also differs

their sins, but the Church as person is not responsible. . . . It is forgotten that the Church as person is the Bride of Christ, 'Whom He has purchased with His own blood' (Acts 20:28)."

("*Toutes les contradictions sont levées . . . dès qu'on a compris que les membres de l'Eglise pèchent, certes, mais en tant qu'ils trahissent l'Eglise; que l'Eglise n'est donc pas sans pécheurs, mais qu'elle est sans péché.*

"*L'Eglise comme personne prend la responsabilité de la pénitence. Elle ne prend pas la responsabilité du péché. . . . Ce sont ses membres eux-mêmes — laiques, clercs, prêtres, évêques, ou papes — qui, en lui désobéissant, prennent la responsabilité du péché; ce n'est pas l'Eglise comme personne. . . . On oublie que l'Eglise comme personne est l'épouse du Christ, 'qu'il se l'est acquise par son propre sang.'* ") Jacques Maritain, *Le paysan de la Garonne* (Paris: Desclée De Brouwer, 1966), 274.

[120]Chicago: Franciscan Herald Press, 1976.

from all other cultural and ethnic traditions. The treasures produced by the Church in the course of history are an outgrowth of the holy life of the Church, manifestations of this life. The theme of Her works is not an idea, a myth, or an ideal of beauty, but Christ the God-man and the history of man's salvation. We are not thinking here of elements relative to a certain epoch, particular habits or decrees of canon law, but of the treasures of Christian culture and Christian spirit that have grown out of the very holy life of the Church. We are thinking of the Gregorian chant, of the hymns and rhythms that exhale in a unique way the world of Christ. Let us mention, for example, the Liturgy of Holy Week, the *Tenebrae*, the *Exsultet*, the Litany of the Saints, the *Veni, Creator Spiritus*, the *Veni, Sancte Spiritus*, the *Dies Irae*, the *Stabat Mater*, or the hymns of St. Thomas Aquinas. Or let us recall the marvelous churches: San Vitale in Ravenna, Hagia Sofia in Istanbul, San Marco in Venice, the Baptistry in Florence, the Cathedral of Chartres, St. Peter's in Rome, and countless others. These are irreplaceable elements of our cultural life.

Church tradition establishes our communion with the past

But from the religious point of view, the cultural tradition of the Church exhibits a completely new dimension — a dimension of communion and community which is an essential part of our Christian ethos and our Christian faith. It is specifically Christian that communion in Christ extends not only to the living members of the Mystical Body of Christ, but also to all those who are either in Purgatory or in Heaven. Thus, for every true Catholic it must be a deeply moving experience to be able to pray the same prayers that the Holy Church has prayed for centuries.

The Catholic spirit of communion extends not only in space; it extends in time. In response to the question, "Who are our real contemporaries?" in the deepest sense of the term, one should answer: "The saints of all times, from St. Peter to St. Pius X, from St. Mary Magdalen to St. Maria Goretti, and all the saints to come." This is so because the saints have a living message of ultimate importance for everyone, a message that testifies to the reality of redemption through Christ and to the change of the face of the earth through the descent of the Holy Spirit on the day of Pentecost.

The Church's tradition cannot be loved too much

No, we have not loved the past too long. We never can love enough the glorious past of the Holy Church, from the very moment of Her birth on Pentecost down to our own days. While deploring all human frailties that appear in Her, all influences exercised by the mentality of the secular city that is trying to invade the Church, we nonetheless cannot wonder enough at the miracle that the very existence of the Church embodies: "One thing I ask of the Lord, this I seek: to dwell in the house of the Lord all the days of my life."[121]

[121] Ps. 26:4 (RSV = Ps. 27:4).

29

The saints

AFTER ALL THAT HAS BEEN SAID, one can hardly be surprised to discover that progressive Catholics have lost interest in the saints and, indeed, exhibit a hostility toward them bordering on resentment. This is a religious degeneration connected with the amoralism that we have previously discussed. It would be a mistake to believe that the new lack of interest in the saints is a mere reaction to some exaggerations and abuses that at times have crept into the veneration of the saints.

The cult of the saints is sometimes exaggerated

Without any doubt, the cult of certain saints has in the past been overemphasized, especially in Latin countries among simple and illiterate people. Certain saints have at times played a greater role in their prayers than the Lord Himself. In their thoughts, in their needs, when they were seeking help from above, they turned primarily to the intercession of a popular saint like St. Anthony or St. Joseph.

Prayers of intercession remain nonetheless important

It is certainly necessary to fight these abuses. But the overemphasis of a good never entitles us to deny the value of the good in question, of its rightful place in the God-given hierarchy of being. Criticism of the exaggerated claims for reason in rationalism, for example, in no way implies the condemnation of reason altogether; on the contrary, this criticism is legitimate only if the high value and God-given status of reason are clearly recognized.

The overemphasis on prayers of intercession to the saints and of the role that a saint plays in religious life does not in the least diminish the significance of prayers of intercession. And still less can it be said to diminish the ineffable gift of God the saints represent and the enormous and essential importance they have in the Mystical Body of Christ.

In Cardinal Newman's comments on the Holy Virgin we find an exemplary way of dealing with the problem.[122] While fighting against a certain overemphasis in the popular devotions of the cult of the Holy Virgin, Newman reverently elaborates the sublime and deeply Catholic veneration of the Mother of God and the unique place she should have in our religious life. He exhibits the same spirit when he speaks about the saints.

Let us therefore not be deceived by the agitation of certain Catholics against the saints and against the important role that they play in the Church. If these Catholics were merely reacting against abuses, then they would adopt an attitude and a procedure similar to Newman's. Rather, they are again manifesting their secularizing penchant.

[122]Letter to Dr. Pusey in *Certain Difficulties Felt by Anglicans in Catholic Teaching Considered*, vol. 2, paragraph 5 (London: Longmans, Green, 1898), 89-170.

Saints show the possibility of our transformation in Christ

Indeed, one of the symptoms of spiritual regression or loss of the *sensus supranaturalis* among progressive Catholics is their attitude toward the saints. They no longer understand the immense importance of the fact that despite all their frailty, human persons have been fully transformed in Christ. The fact of "the existence of those rare servants of God who rise up from time to time in the Catholic Church like angels in disguise, and shed around them a light, as they walk on their way heavenward"[123] is proof that Christ really has redeemed the world and that the Holy Spirit descended on the faithful on the day of Pentecost. One saint alone would suffice to prove the reality of these events because his holiness could never be explained on a purely natural level.

Every saint whose personality clearly manifests his transformation in Christ, who exhibits the quality of holiness with its supernatural perfume and splendor, is proof that notwithstanding all our misery and sinfulness, we, too, can attain a full transformation in Christ. The saints have not only converted innumerable people by their very being, they have also caused many to ask with St. Augustine: "If these can [achieve holiness], then why not I?"

Saints glorify God

Every saint is a realization of the kingdom of God for which we pray in the Our Father; for in him grace has brought forth all its fruits and in his personality the Sacred Humanity of Christ is reflected. One saint thus glorifies God more than all the improvements of man's earthly welfare ever could, to say nothing of

[123]John Henry Cardinal Newman, *Discourses Addressed to Mixed Congregations* (London: Longmans, Green, 1921), 94.

"evolutionary processes" or "cosmic events." Moreover, every saint is an incredible gift to us from God. We are privileged to witness Christ's triumph in a human being, to taste the very essence of holiness. Any man who does not experience this as a wonderful gift, who is not inebriated by the fact that in every saint's personality we are granted a glimpse of the supernatural glory, does not really love Christ and is no real Catholic.

Saints challenge us to grow holy

For many Catholics who proudly call themselves progressives, purely humanitarian activities and social institutions are more attractive than holiness. They have become blind to the light of Christ. Further, the ideal they have chosen is far removed from the challenge that every saint embodies. Striving for social justice — good and honorable as it is — does not presuppose that we die to ourselves, that we break with the spirit of the world, that we renounce Satan and the pomp of this world. But every saint, by the resplendent fact of his holiness, shakes our consciences and calls us also to renounce the world and its pomp.

The saints are an uncomfortable challenge to those who do not thirst for holiness. Because these progressive Catholics do not want their complacency disturbed, because they do not wish to be drawn out of the ghetto of the "secular city," they want to eliminate the saints. The saints bring the supernatural uncomfortably near. They confront us with the ethos of holiness and disturb those who interpret the Christian life according to their own fashion.

Saints demonstrate that holiness is possible

All those who show no interest in the existence of saints, who try to exclude the saints as much as possible from the life of the

Church, only demonstrate that something is wrong with their relation to Christ. We should not forget that the Church's doctrine of justification insists on the possibility of men being fully transformed in Christ, of their becoming saints. It is here that the deepest differences between the Catholic Church and Luther's doctrine of *sola fides* is to be found. The possibility of becoming a saint is profoundly connected with the Catholic conception of original sin, with the collaboration with grace to which every baptized person is called, with freedom of will, and many other fundamental elements of the deposit of Catholic faith. If a man is not concerned about this central point of Catholic doctrine, he exhibits a serious symptom of the loss of genuine faith.

Secularism minimizes attention to the saints

It is not simply a misconceived ecumenism directed at the Protestants that is at the basis of this tendency to eliminate the saints or minimize their importance.

Deplorable as it is to falsify Catholic doctrine in order to efface the difference separating Catholics from Protestantism, there is much more behind the contemporary antipathy to the saints. It involves, as we indicated above, the loss of the *sensus supranaturalis* and the infection of secularism. And, in all truth, this secularism is a greater obstacle to communion with orthodox Protestants than is the veneration of saints.

God wills us to pray to the saints

Another aspect of the position of saints in the Church must be mentioned: the grand, beautiful, and authentically Catholic intercession of the saints on behalf of the faithful. The belief that those who are united with God forever in eternity, in full possession of the beatific vision, are able to intercede for us — indeed, are *called* to intercede — is rooted in the deep communion that exists between the militant, the suffering, and the triumphant Church. A glorious manifestation of the indestructible bond of union in Christ and of Christian charity is given in the fact that we can address ourselves to the saints and ask for their intercession. The inexhaustible love with which the saints embraced their brethren during their lives on earth does not cease at their death. Such is the strength of the bond that unites them to their brethren in Christ.

The objection that God does not need this intercession is as illogical as it is irrelevant. Undoubtedly, God does not need such intercession in order to hear our prayers. But the question of whether God "needs" something implies a false anthropomorphism. God in His omnipotence needs nothing. The question that matters is whether God has willed it so. If He has, then our task is to appreciate the infinite beauty and glory of the gifts He has willed. The ways God has chosen for the salvation of mankind are not the expression of a necessity, but of His infinite love. Thus, for all who perceive the glorious beauty of the communion of saints, of the Mystical Body of Christ, of the fact that the saints in heaven lovingly intercede for us, the question of whether it is necessary is beside the point. This intercession is certainly not indispensable or essential to our salvation, and God could have instituted it otherwise. But we should praise Him for the intercession of saints, a free gift of His ineffable love.

The saints do not interfere with worship of God

Equally invalid is the argument that holds that by admitting the intercession of saints, by addressing ourselves to them, we have interfered with the direct relation of the Christian to God in

Christ, that we have erected a "screen" between God and ourselves. This would be true if we no longer prayed directly to God or to Christ the God-man, and all our prayers were addressed to saints. But this is not the case. Not only is our adoration directed exclusively to God and Christ, but all the prayers of praise as well. In the main act of cult — the Holy Sacrifice of the Mass — we are directed solely to God through Christ: "Through Him, with Him, and in Him." The petition prayers are also primarily addressed directly to God. The prayers addressed to the saints, such as the marvelous Litany of the Saints, in which we invoke their intercession on our behalf before God, are only lovely blossoms growing out of and surrounding the essential prayer in which God is addressed directly. This is clearly expressed in the Liturgy of every feast of a saint.

It should not be necessary to insist in this context on the unique position of the Blessed Virgin Mary. Her connection with Christ and the salvation of mankind cannot be compared with that of any other saint. All that has been said about prayers to the saints applies all the more to the Holy Virgin.

Veneration is due to the saints

Veneration of the saints is clearly a consequence of our loving adoration of Christ. Everyone whose heart has been touched by the Sacred Humanity of Christ, by His ineffable holiness and supernatural beauty, cannot but be attracted by those men and women who have been transformed in Him and in whom we find a reflection of His holiness. "But to me thy friends, O God, are made exceedingly honourable."[124] This veneration, this special act

[124]Ps. 138:17 in the Douay-Rheims edition. The RSV (Ps. 139:17) translates the passage as "How precious to me are thy thoughts, O God!"

of reverent admiration, is the value response due to the saint. It is worlds away from adoration, which is essentially a response to the Absolute Person. It is also completely different from any kind of veneration, admiration, or esteem that constitutes our response to personalities endowed with high natural values such as moral and intellectual gifts. It is a religious veneration, a response only due to someone who reflects the Sacred Humanity of Christ, one endowed with all the fruits of grace.

30

Epilogue

WE HAVE MENTIONED time and again the disastrous idea of adapting Christ's message to the modern world. If, as Hans Urs von Balthasar puts it, " 'modern man' (indeed, a mythical entity) becomes the measure for what God has or has not to say," then religion is obviously at an end.[125]

True renewal calls us to transformation in Christ

Christ cannot but be a scandal for the world in all epochs of history, because an essential antagonism exists between the spirit of Christ and the spirit of the world. True renewal of the Church, as Urs von Balthasar points out, consists in eliminating what is false in the Church — unchristian scandals — in order to throw into relief the true *scandal* of the Church that is rooted in Her very mission.

[125] Hans Urs von Balthasar, *Wer ist ein Christ?*, 4th ed. (Zurich: Benziger, 1966), 35.

No slogans about the sentimentality and devotionalism of former times can deceive one who has eyes to see and ears to hear about the never changing nature of the authentic meaning and vocation of our life: to be transformed in Christ and to glorify God by attaining holiness. No appeal to the *Kairos* can make the true Christian doubt the perennial validity of Christ's words to Martha: "Martha, Martha, thou art careful and art troubled about many things, but one thing only is necessary."[126]

To those who claim that the time for contemplation is passed and that he who looks up at the skies "romantically" will see nothing but fuming chimneys (for today we supposedly can only find God in the midst of action), Urs von Balthasar replies that he who does not listen to God has nothing to say to the world. He will, as do so many priests and laymen today, care for many things to the point of exhaustion, and yet miss the one thing necessary.[127]

No criticism of the Council of Trent, no pharisaical feeling of superiority to the Catholicism of the nineteenth century, no stress on activism or the idea of adoring God through doing business, through leaving the pale of devotionalism, can blur for the true Christian the ultimate validity of the words of St. Paul: "Seek the things that are above."[128] He will clearly see the antithesis between Christ and the world. The sublime liturgy of Baptism will retain for him its full validity and existential realism:

Do you renounce Satan? *I do.*
And all his works? *I do.*
And all his pomp? *I do.*

[126]Luke 10:41-42.
[127]Von Balthasar, *Wer ist ein Christ?*, 83.
[128]Col. 3:1.

Epilogue

This book has been written out of a deep sorrow at witnessing the emergence of false prophets within the City of God. It is sad enough when people lose their faith and leave the Church; but it is much worse when those who in reality have lost their faith remain within the Church and try — like termites — to undermine Christian faith with their claim that they are giving to Christian revelation the interpretation that suits "modern man."

I wish to conclude this book with an appeal to all those whose faith is not corroded to beware of these false prophets who want to extradite Christ to the secular city in a way analogous to Judas' betrayal of Jesus into the hands of His persecutors.

The teachings of the false prophets

Let us recall the marks of these false prophets. He is a false prophet who denies original sin and mankind's need of redemption and thereby undermines the meaning of Christ's death on the Cross. He is not a true Christian who no longer sees that redemption of the world through Christ is the source of true happiness and that nothing can be compared to this one glorious fact.

He is a false prophet who no longer accepts the absolute primacy of the first commandment of Christ — to love God above all things — and who claims that our love of God can manifest itself exclusively in our love of neighbor. He is a false prophet who no longer understands that to long for the *I-Thou* union with Christ and for transformation in Christ is the very meaning of our life. He is a false prophet who claims that morality reveals itself not primarily in man's relationship with God, but in those things that concern human welfare. And he has fallen prey to the teaching of false prophets who only sees in the wrong done our neighbor our injury to him and remains blind to the offense against God that this wrong implies.

He who no longer sees the radical difference that exists between charity and humanitarian benevolence has become deaf to the message of Christ.

He who is more impressed and thrilled by "cosmic processes," "evolution," and the speculations of science than by the reflection of Christ's Sacred Humanity in a saint and by the victory over the world that the very existence of a saint embodies, is no longer filled with the Christian spirit. He who cares more for the earthly welfare of humanity than for its sanctification has lost the Christian view of the universe. As Cardinal Newman said:

> The Church aims, not at making a show, but at doing a work. She regards this world, and all that is in it, as a mere shadow, as dust and ashes, compared with the value of one single soul. She holds that unless She can, in Her own way, do good to souls, it is no use Her doing anything. . . . She considers the action of this world and the action of the soul simply incommensurate, viewed in their respective spheres; She would rather save the soul of one single wild bandit of Calabria or whining beggar of Palermo, than draw a hundred lines of railroad through the length and breadth of Italy, or carry out a sanitary reform, in its fullest details, in every city of Sicily, except so far as these great national works tended to some spiritual good beyond them.[129]

Beware of false prophets who ignore the repeated warnings of our Holy Father, Pope Paul VI, as well as the Holy See's clear formulation of the various heresies and misconceptions pervading the world today. Beware of those who try to drown the voice of the Vicar of Christ in noisy propaganda.

[129]John Henry Cardinal Newman, *Certain Difficulties Felt by Anglicans in Catholic Teaching Considered*, vol. 1 (London: Longmans, 1908), 239-40.

Epilogue

There are profound reasons for hope

Nevertheless, as I said at the beginning of this book, if my heart bleeds from seeing the ravages done in the vineyard of the Lord and from seeing the defilement of the sanctuary of the Church, I am yet full of hope, because our Lord has said: "The gates of Hell shall not prevail against it."[130]

Without a trace of optimism, but full of hope and love for the Holy Church, for the Mystical Body of Christ, for the City of God, and in a spirit of deep devotion and obedience to our Holy Father, Pope Paul VI, who has admonished us in this year of faith to pray the Nicene Creed, let me conclude with the words of this credo:

I believe in one, holy,
catholic and apostolic
Church.

[130]Matt. 16:18.

Biographical note

Dietrich von Hildebrand (1889-1977)

HITLER FEARED HIM and the late Pope Pius XII called him "the twentieth-century Doctor of the Church." For more than six decades, Dietrich von Hildebrand — philosopher, spiritual writer, and anti-Nazi crusader — led philosophical, religious, and political groups, lectured throughout Europe and the Americas, and published more than thirty books and many more articles. His influence was widespread and endures to this day.

Although von Hildebrand was a deep and original thinker on subjects ranging across the spectrum of human interests, still, in his lectures and his writings, he instinctively avoided extravagant speculations and convoluted theories. Instead, he sought to illuminate the nature and significance of seemingly *everyday* elements of human existence that are easily misunderstood and too frequently taken for granted. Therefore, much of von Hildebrand's philosophy concerns the human person, the person's interior ethical and affective life, and the relations that should exist between the person and the world in which he finds himself.

Von Hildebrand's background made him uniquely qualified to examine these topics. He was born in beautiful Florence in 1889, the son of the renowned German sculptor, Adolf von Hildebrand. At the time, the von Hildebrand home was a center of art and culture, visited by the greatest European artists and musicians of the day. Young Dietrich's early acquaintance with these vibrant, creative people intensified his natural zest for life.

In Florence, von Hildebrand was surrounded by beauty — the overwhelming natural beauty of the Florentine countryside and the rich beauty of the many art treasures that are Florence's Renaissance heritage. Pervading this Florentine atmosphere was Catholicism: in the art, in the architecture, and in the daily life of the people. These early years in Florence quickened in the young von Hildebrand a passionate love of truth, of goodness, of beauty, and of Christianity.

As he grew older, he developed a profound love for philosophy, studying under some of the greatest of this century's German philosophers, including Edmund Husserl, Max Scheler, and Adolf Reinach. Converting to Catholicism in 1914, von Hildebrand taught philosophy for many years at the University of Munich.

However, soon after the end of World War I, Nazism began to threaten von Hildebrand's beloved southern Germany. With his characteristic clear-sightedness, von Hildebrand immediately discerned its intrinsic evil. From its earliest days, he vociferously denounced Nazism in his articles and in speeches throughout Germany and the rest of Europe.

Declaring himself unwilling to continue to live in a country ruled by a criminal, von Hildebrand regretfully left his native Germany for Austria, where he continued teaching philosophy (at the University of Vienna) and fought the Nazis with even greater vigor, founding and then publishing for a number of years a prominent anti-Nazi newspaper, *Christliche Ständestaat*.

This angered both Heinrich Himmler and Adolf Hitler, who were determined to silence von Hildebrand and to close his anti-Nazi newspaper. Orders were given to have him assassinated in Austria. However, von Hildebrand evaded the hit-squads and, thanks to his Swiss passport, was finally able to flee the country just as it fell to the Nazis.

It is typical of von Hildebrand that even while he was engaged in this dangerous life-and-death struggle against the Nazis, he maintained his deep spiritual life and managed to write during this period his greatest work, the sublime and highly acclaimed spiritual classic, *Transformation in Christ*.

Fleeing from Austria, von Hildebrand was pursued through many countries, ultimately arriving on the shores of America in 1940 by way of France, Spain, Portugal, and Brazil.

Penniless in New York after his heroic struggle against the Nazis, von Hildebrand was hired as a professor of philosophy at Fordham University where he taught until his retirement. Many of his best works were written during this period and after his retirement. He died in 1977 in New Rochelle, New York.

Dietrich von Hildebrand was remarkable for his keen intellect, his profound originality, his prodigious output, his great personal courage, his deep spirituality, and his intense love of truth, goodness, and beauty. These rare qualities made Dietrich von Hildebrand one of the greatest philosophers and one of the wisest men of the twentieth century.

Appendix

Teilhard de Chardin: a false prophet

I MET TEILHARD DE CHARDIN in 1949 at a dinner arranged by Father Robert Gannon, S.J., then president of Fordham University. Previously, the noted scholars Father Henri de Lubac and Msgr. Bruno de Solages had highly recommended him to me. I was, therefore, full of expectations. After the meal, Father Teilhard delivered a long exposition of his views.

Teilhard's lecture was a great disappointment, for it manifested utter philosophical confusion, especially in his conception of the human person. I was even more upset by his theological primitiveness. He ignored completely the decisive difference between nature and supernature. After a lively discussion in which I ventured a criticism of his ideas, I had an opportunity to speak to Teilhard privately. When our talk touched on St. Augustine, he exclaimed violently: "Don't mention that unfortunate man; he spoiled everything by introducing the supernatural." This remark confirmed the impression I had gained of the crass naturalism of his views, but it also struck me another way. The criticism of St. Augustine, the greatest of the Fathers of the Church, betrayed Teilhard's lack of a genuine sense of intellectual and spiritual grandeur.

It was only after reading several of his works, however, that I fully realized the catastrophic implications of his philosophical ideas and saw the absolute incompatibility of his theology fiction with Christian revelation and with the doctrine of the Church.

Teilhard was not a careful scientist

Many Catholics view Teilhard de Chardin as a great scientist who has reconciled science with the Christian faith by introducing a grandiose new theology and metaphysics that take modern scientific findings into account and thus fit into our scientific age. Although I am not a competent judge of Teilhard as a scientist, this opinion may be questioned without expertise. For one thing, every careful thinker knows that a reconciliation of science and the Christian faith has never been needed, because true science (in contradistinction to false philosophies disguised in scientific garments) can never be incompatible with Christian faith. Science can neither prove nor disprove the truth of the faith. Let us also note several evaluations of Teilhard by outstanding scientists.

Jean Rostand has said of Teilhard's works: "I have argued that Teilhard did not cast the slightest light on the great problem of organic evolution."[131] Sir Peter Medawar, the Nobel Prize winner, speaks of Teilhard's mental confusion and the exaggerated expression that borders, he says, on hysteria. He insists that *The Phenomenon of Man* is unscientific in its procedure. Sir Peter adds that Teilhard's works in general lack scientific structure, that his competence in his field is modest, that he neither knows what a

[131] *Figaro Littéraire*, 23-29 September 1965.

logical argument is nor what a scientific proof is, and that he does not respect the norms required for scientific scholarship.[132]

Thus, since the halo surrounding Teilhard is not unrelated to the opinion that he was a great scientist, it should be noted that his scientific accomplishments are, at the very least, controversial. My purpose here, however, is to examine Teilhard's philosophical and theological thought and its bearings on Christian revelation and the doctrine of the Church. I wish to make it clear from the beginning that writing on Teilhard is no easy matter. I do not know of another thinker who so artfully jumps from one position to another contradictory one, without being disturbed by the jump or even noticing it. One is driven therefore to speak of the underlying trend of his thought, to identify the logical consequences of the core of his doctrine — of what was dearest to him.

Teilhard fails to grasp the nature of the person

One of the most striking philosophical shortcomings of Teilhard's system is his conception of man. It is a great irony that the author of *The Phenomenon of Man* should completely miss the nature of man as a person. He fails to recognize the abyss separating a person from the entire impersonal world around him, the wholly new dimension of being that a person implies.

Teilhard sees "self-consciousness" as the only difference between man and a highly developed animal. Nonetheless, a comparison of the limited type of consciousness that can be observed in animals with the manifold aspects of a person's consciousness shows instantly how wrong it is to regard the latter as merely an addition of self-consciousness. Personal consciousness actualizes

[132]*Mind* 70 (1961): 99-106. See also the collection of articles in "Teilhard et la science," *Itinéraires*, No. 96 (1965).

itself in knowledge — in the luminous consciousness of an object that reveals itself to our mind, in the capacity to adapt our mind to the nature of the object (*adequatio intellectus ad rem*), in an understanding of the object's nature. It also actualizes itself in the process of inference, in the capacity to ask questions, to pursue truth, and last, but not least, in the capacity to develop an *I-thou* communion with another person. All of this implies a completely new type of consciousness, an entirely new dimension of being.

But this marvel of the human mind, which is also revealed in language and in man's role as *homo pictor* (imaginative man, man as artist), is altogether lost on Teilhard because he insists on viewing human consciousness as merely an *awareness* of self that has gradually developed out of animal consciousness.

The scholastics, on the other hand, accurately grasped the dimensions of personal consciousness by calling the person a being that *possesses* itself. Compared with the person, every impersonal being *sleeps*, as it were; it simply endures its existence. Only in the human person do we find an awakened being, a being truly possessing itself, notwithstanding its contingency.

Teilhardian "fusion" of persons is impossible

Teilhard's failure to appreciate the person again comes to the fore when he claims in *The Phenomenon of Man* that a collective consciousness would constitute a higher state of evolution:

> The idea is that the earth would not only become covered by myriads of grains of thought but enclosed in a single thinking envelope so as to form, functionally, no more than a single vast grain of thought on the sidereal scale.[133]

[133] *The Phenomenon of Man* (New York: Harper, 1967), 251.

Here several grave errors combine. First, a non-individual consciousness is contradictory. Second, it is wrong to suppose that this impossible fiction could contain something superior to individual personal existence. Third, the idea of a "superconsciousness" is, in fact, a totalitarian ideal; it implies an absolute antithesis to true community, which essentially presupposes individual persons.

The existence of a human person is so essentially individual that the idea of fusing two persons into one or splitting one into two is radically impossible. It is also impossible to wish to be another person. We can only wish to be *like* another person. For at the moment we became the other person we would necessarily cease to exist. It belongs to the very nature of the human being as person that he remain this one individual being. God could annihilate him, though revelation tells us that this is not God's intention. But the supposition that a human being could give up his individual character without ceasing to exist, without being annihilated by that act, amounts to blindness to what a person is.

Some men claim to experience a kind of "union with the cosmos" which "enlarges" their individual existence and presents itself as the acquisition of a "superconsciousness." In reality, however, this union exists only in the consciousness of the individual person who has such an experience. Its content — the feeling of fusion with the cosmos — is in fact the peculiar experience of one concrete person, and in no way implies a collective consciousness.

Our consideration of Teilhard's ideal of "collective man" reveals that he fails to understand not only the nature of man as person but also the nature of true communion and community. True personal communion, in which we attain union much deeper than any ontological fusion, presupposes the favorable individual character of the person. Compared to the union achieved by the conscious interpenetration of souls in mutual love, the fusion of impersonal beings is nothing more than juxtaposition.

Teilhard does not recognize the hierarchy of being

Teilhard's ideal of "superhumanity" — his totalitarian conception of community — shows the same naive ignorance of the abyss that separates the glorious realm of personal existence from the impersonal world. It also reveals his blindness to the hierarchy of being and to the hierarchy of values. Pascal admirably illuminated the incomparable superiority of one individual person to the entire impersonal world when to his famous remark, "Man is but a reed, the most feeble thing in nature," he added, "but if the universe were to crush him, man would still be more noble than that which killed him. He knows that he dies, and the advantage which the universe has over him. The universe knows nothing of this."[134]

Another aspect of Teilhard's blindness to the essentially individual character of the person is his inordinate interest in man as species. Again he overlooks the differences between humans and mere animals. A dominant interest in the species is normal as long as one deals with animals, but it becomes grotesque when human beings are involved. Kierkegaard brought out this point when he stressed the absolute superiority of the individual human being to the human species.[135] Teilhard's own approach is betrayed by his attitude toward the atomic bombing of Hiroshima. The "progress" of humanity which he sees in the invention of nuclear weapons matters more to him than the destruction of innumerable lives and the most terrible sufferings inflicted on individual persons.

[134]Blaise Pascal, *Pensées*, trans. W. F. Trotter, vol. 33 of *The Great Books of the Western World* (Chicago: Encyclopaedia Britannica, 1952), VI, 347.

[135]"In the animal world, the 'individual' is always less important than the race. But it is a peculiarity of the human race that just because the individual is created in the image of God, the 'individual' is above the race." From a journal entry for 1850 in Alexander Dru, ed., *The Journals of Kierkegaard* (N.Y.: Harper and Row, 1958), 187.

It is true that time and again Teilhard speaks of the personal and of the superiority of the personal over the impersonal. Indeed, he often explicitly rejects the possibility that the existence of the individual person will dissolve. He writes, for instance, in *Building the Earth*: "Since there is neither fusion nor dissolution of individual persons, the center which they aspire to reach must necessarily be distinct from them, that is, it must have its own personality, its autonomous reality." Yet just a few pages later we find him rhapsodizing: "And lastly the totalization of the individual in the collective man." Teilhard then explains how this contradiction will dissolve in the Omega: "All these so-called impossibilities come about under the influence of love."[136]

Teilhard tries to eliminate antitheses

It has recently become fashionable to accept contradictions as a sign of philosophical depth. Mutually contradictory elements are regarded as antagonistic as long as the discussion remains on a logical level, but are considered unimportant as soon as it reaches the religious sphere. This fashion does not do away with the essential impossibility of combining contradictories. No number of modish paradoxes, of emotional effusions, of exotically capitalized words can conceal Teilhard's fundamental lack of understanding of the nature of the person. The notion of the "personal" in Teilhard's system is stripped of any real meaning by the system's underlying pantheism. In Teilhard's thought, "collective man" and the "totalization" of man represent an ideal that is objectively incompatible with the existence of the individual person — or rather, that necessarily implies the annihilation of the person.

[136] *Building the Earth* (Wilkes-Barre, Penn.: Dimension Books, 1965), 79, 83.

His monistic tendency leads him to try to liquidate all real antitheses. He wants to keep the integrity of the person, but raves about totalization. He reduces all contraries to different aspects of the same thing and then claims that the antithetical nature of the propositions in question is due merely to the isolation or overemphasis of a single aspect. Yet by reading Teilhard closely, one can always detect his primary concern and see where he is going.

A passage comparing democracy, communism, and fascism in *Building the Earth* illustrates this. A superficial reading of the passage (which, incidentally, contains several excellent remarks) might give the impression that Teilhard does not deny the individual character of man. A closer, critical study against the background of other passages clearly reveals not only an impossible attempt to unite individuality and totalization, but also Teilhard's intention, what his main ideal is, where his heart is. It is, once again, with totalization, with superhumanity in the Omega.[137]

Teilhard misunderstands communion and community

The penchant for liquidating antitheses also sheds light on Teilhard's false conception of community. It is all conceived upon the pattern of fusion in the realm of matter, and thus misses the radical difference between unification in the sphere of matter and the spiritual union that comes to pass through real love in the sphere of individual persons. For Teilhard, love is merely cosmic energy: "That energy which, having generally agitated the cosmic mass, emerges from it to form the Noosphere, what name must be given to such an influence? One only — love."[138] A man who can write that has failed to grasp the nature of this supreme act which,

[137]Ibid., 24-32.
[138]Ibid., 82.

by its very essence, presupposes the existence both of a conscious, personal being and a *thou*.

Teilhard leaves no place for love

There is no place in the unanimity and harmony of Teilhard's totalitarian communion for a real giving of oneself in love. This unanimity and harmony is actualized through a convergence into one mind; it thus differs radically from the *concordia*, from the blissful union of which the Liturgy of the Mandatum speaks: "The love of Christ has gathered us into one." The latter is not a "co-thinking," but rather a mutual, reciprocal love and a unification in Christ based on the personal love-response which every individual gives to Christ.

In a monistic world, there is absolutely no place for the *intentio unionis* (the intention of union) and the *intentio benevolentiae* (good will) proper to real love. For in such a monistic world "cosmic energy" moves everything independently of man's free response. When we interpret things that are merely analogous as constituting an ontological unity, or when we use as literal and univocal a term that is analogous, we necessarily bar the way to a real understanding of the being in question. Every monism is ultimately nihilistic.

Teilhard misses the difference between matter and spirit

Another grave philosophical error is closely linked to Teilhard's conception of man: his failure to grasp the radical difference between spirit and matter. Teilhard deals with energy as though it were a genus and then proceeds to make matter and spirit two distinct species in this genus. But there is no genus of energy. Energy is a concept applicable to both of these radically different realms of being only in terms of analogy. Teilhard does not understand this; he even speaks of the "spiritual power of matter."[139]

Teilhard forces reality to fit into his system

Teilhard, then, indulges in constructions and hypotheses without caring much about what is "given." Maritain once said: "The main difference between philosophers is whether they see or do not see." Teilhard employs much imagination but no intuition, no listening to experience. From this comes his attempt to project consciousness into inanimate matter, for which there is simply no foundation apart from his desire to erect a monistic system. Instead of listening to experience, to the voice of being, he arbitrarily infuses into the being in question whatever corresponds to his system. It is indeed surprising that a man who attacks traditional philosophy and theology for abstractness and for trying to adjust reality to a closed system should himself offer the most abstract and unrealistic system imaginable into which he attempts to force reality. He thereby follows the famous example of Procrustes.[140]

The ambiguity underlying Teilhard's thought also emerges in a passage that accuses Communism of being too materialistic, of striving only for the progress of matter and, consequently, ignoring spiritual progress. His admirers might point to this passage as proof

[139]"As you know, I have always been attracted by the idea of writing a hymn 'to the spiritual power of Matter.' " *The Making of a Mind: Letters from a Soldier-Priest* (New York: Harper, 1965), 292.

[140]Procrustes was a notorious figure from classical mythology who lived in a house on the road that ran between the Greek cities of Eleusis and Athens. Procrustes, whose name means "Stretcher," would invite travelers to stay with him, and if they did not fit exactly into his bed, he would either stretch them or cut off their limbs until they did!

that Teilhard clearly distinguishes between matter and spirit and acknowledges the superiority of the latter.

Actually, it proves no such thing. Teilhard always distinguishes between matter and spirit, but he regards them as merely two stages in the evolutionary process. Physical energy becomes — is transformed into — spiritual energy. But to regard the difference between the two as simply stages of a process — or, as we may put it, to regard the difference as a "gradual" one — is utterly to fail to understand the nature of the spirit. Again, monism prevents an understanding of reality and creates the illusion of being able to combine what cannot be combined.

Teilhard implicitly denies man has free will

Teilhard's incomprehension of man's nature is further evidenced in his implicit denial of man's free will.[141] By grounding man's spiritual life in an evolutionary process which by definition acts independently of man's free will and transcends the person, Teilhard clearly denies the decisive role of human freedom. Freedom of will is obviously one of the most significant and deepest marks of a person. Thus, once again, he overlooks the radical difference between man as person and a highly developed animal.

The role of freedom of will emerges decisively in man's capacity to bear moral values and disvalues. This highest characteristic of man presupposes free will and responsibility. Nonetheless, Teilhard blithely reduces the antithesis between good and evil to mere stages of evolution, to mere degrees of perfection — surely a classic case of philosophical impotence. Moreover, he ignores the critical importance of the moral question strikingly expressed in Socrates'

[141] "The moral and social development of Humanity is the authentic, 'natural' consequence of organic evolution." *The Making of a Mind*, 110-11.

immortal dictum: "It is better for man to suffer injustice than to commit it."[142] In Teilhard, the entire drama of man's existence, the fight between good and evil in his soul, is ignored or, rather, overshadowed by evolutionary growth toward the Omega.

Teilhardism and Christianity are incompatible

Teilhard's thought is thus hopelessly at odds with Christianity. Christian revelation presupposes certain basic natural facts such as the existence of objective truth, the spiritual reality of an individual person, the radical difference between spirit and matter, the difference between body and soul, the unalterable objectivity of moral good and evil, freedom of the will, the immortality of the soul, and, of course, the existence of a personal God. Teilhard's approach to all of these questions reveals an unbridgeable chasm between his theology fiction and Christian revelation.

Teilhard adapts religion to modern man

This conclusion inescapably follows from Teilhard's frequently repeated arguments for a new interpretation of Christianity. Time and again he argues that we can no longer expect modern man, living in an industrialized world and in the scientific age, to accept Christian doctrine as it has been taught for the last two thousand years. Teilhard's new interpretation of Christianity is fashioned by asking, "What fits into our modern world?" This approach combines historical relativism and pragmatism with a radical blindness to the very essence of religion.

We have considered the myth of modern man throughout this book. It suffices here to insist that man always remains essentially

[142] Plato, *Gorgias* 469c, 527b.

the same with regard to his moral dangers, his moral obligations, his need of redemption, and the true sources of his happiness. We have also examined the catastrophic error of historical relativism, which confuses the socio-historical aliveness of an idea with its validity and truth. If it is nonsense to claim that a basic natural truth can be true in the Middle Ages but is no longer so in our time, the absurdity is even greater when the subject is religion.

With a religion the only question that matters is whether it is true. The question of whether or not it fits into the mentality of an epoch cannot play any role in the acceptance or the rejection of a religion without betraying the very essence of religion. Even the earnest atheist recognizes this. He will not say that today we can no longer believe in God; he will say that God is and always was a mere illusion. From the position that a religion must be adapted to the spirit of an epoch there is but a short step to the absurd drivel (which we associate with Bertrand Russell or the Nazi ideologist Bergmann) about having to invent a new religion.

In a 1952 letter Teilhard wrote: "As I love to say, the synthesis of the Christian God (of the *above*) and the Marxist God (of the *forward*) — Behold! That is the only God whom henceforth we can adore in spirit and in truth."[143] In these remarks the abyss separating Teilhard from Christianity is manifest in every word. To speak of a "Marxist God" is very surprising and would never have been accepted by Marx. But the idea of a synthesis of the Christian God with an alleged Marxist God, as well as the simultaneous application of the term *God* to Christianity and to Marxism,

[143]Letter from New York, April 2, 1952. As quoted in Roger Garaudy, "Le Père Teilhard, le concile et les marxistes," *Europe*, No. 431-32 (1965): 206. This issue of *Europe* is devoted to Teilhard. Most of the studies are sympathetic, and for this reason they often succeed in revealing the true direction of Teilhard's thought. The issue also contains a number of previously unpublished manuscipts of Teilhard.

demonstrates the absolute incompatibility of Teilhard's thought with the doctrine of the Church. Note, moreover, the words "henceforth" and "can." They are the key to Teilhard's thinking and expose unmistakably his historical relativism.

Teilhard's Christ is not the Christ of the Gospels

In *Le paysan de la Garonne*, Jacques Maritain remarks that Teilhard is most anxious to preserve Christ. But, adds Maritain, "What a Christ!"[144] It is here, indeed, that we find the most radical difference between the doctrine of the Church and Teilhard de Chardin's theology fiction. Teilhard's Christ is no longer Jesus, the God-man, the epiphany of God, the Redeemer. Instead, He is the initiator of a purely natural evolutionary process and, simultaneously, its end — the Christ-Omega. An unprejudiced mind cannot but ask: why should this "cosmic force" be called Christ?

It would be utter naiveté to be misled by the fact that Teilhard labels this alleged cosmogenic force *Christ* or by his desperate effort to wrap this pantheism in traditional Catholic terms. In his basic conception of the world, which does not provide for original sin in the sense the Church gives to this term, there is no place for the Jesus Christ of the Gospels; for if there is no original sin, the redemption of man through Christ loses its inner meaning.

In Christian revelation, stress is laid on the sanctification and salvation of every individual person, leading to the beatific vision and, simultaneously, to the communion of saints. In Teilhard's theology, stress is laid on the progress of the earth, the evolution leading to Christ-Omega. Salvation through Christ's death has no place since man's destiny is part of pancosmic evolution.

[144] *Le paysan de la Garonne*, 173-87, 383-90.

Teilhard redefines basic Christian doctrine

Teilhard's conception of man, implicit denial of free will, tacit amoralism, and totalitarian collectivism cut him off from Christian revelation — and this notwithstanding his efforts to reconcile his views with Church teaching. He writes: "Yes, the moral and social development of humanity is indeed the authentic and natural consequence of organic evolution." For such a man, original sin, redemption, and sanctification no longer have real meaning. Yet Teilhard does not seem quite aware of this incompatibility:

> Sometimes I am a bit afraid when I think of the transposition to which I must submit my mind concerning the vulgar notions of creation, inspiration, miracle, original sin, resurrection, etc., in order to be able to accept them.[145]

That Teilhard applies the term *vulgar*, even if not in the pejorative sense, to the basic elements of Christian revelation and to their interpretation by the infallible magisterium of the Church should suffice to disclose the gnostic and esoteric character of his thought. He writes to Leontine Zanta:

> As you know, what dominates my interest and my preoccupations is the effort to establish in myself and to spread around a new religion (you may call it a better Christianity) in which the personal God ceases to be the great neolithic proprietor of former times, in order to become the soul of the world; our religious and cultural stage calls for this.[146]

[145]Letter of December 17, 1922, in *Lettres*, No. 49-50 (1962), 36. As quoted in Philippe de la Trinité, *Rome et Teilhard de Chardin* (Paris: Arthème Fayard, 1964), 47.

[146]*Lettres à Léontine Zanta* (Paris: Desclée De Brouwer, 1965). As quoted in Maritain, *Le paysan de la Garonne*, 175.

Not only, then, is the Christ of the Gospels replaced by a Christ-Omega, but also the God of the old and new covenants is replaced by a pantheistic God, "the soul of the world"—and again on the strength of the unfortunate argument that God must be adapted to the man of our scientific age.

Teilhard banishes grace and the supernatural

No wonder Teilhard reproaches St. Augustine for introducing the difference between the natural and supernatural. In Teilhard's pantheistic, naturalistic "religion" there is no place for the supernatural or the world of grace. Rather, union with God consists principally in assimilation into an evolutionary process, not in the supernatural life of grace infused in our souls through Baptism.

Why does the one tend to exclude the other? If Teilhard's notion of a participation in an evolutionary process were reality, it could only be a form of *concursus divinus*. Yet great and mysterious as is the *concursus divinus*—that is, the support God gives at every moment of our natural existence, without which we would sink back into nothingness—there is an abyss separating this *natural* metaphysical contact from grace.

Whether or not Teilhard explicitly denies the reality of grace does not matter much. His ecstasy about the natural contact with God in the alleged evolutionary process clearly discloses the subordinate role, if any, that he assigns to grace. To put it otherwise: after Teilhard has replaced the personal God, Creator of heaven and earth, by God the soul of the world, after he has transformed the Christ of the Gospels into the Christ-Omega, after he has replaced redemption by a natural evolutionary process, what is *left* for grace? Maritain makes the point admirably. After granting that Teilhard's spectacle of a divine movement of creation toward God does not lack grandeur, he observes:

> But what does he tell us about the secret path that matters more for us than any spectacle? What can he tell us of the essential, the mystery of the Cross and the redeeming blood, as well as of the grace, the presence of which in one single soul has more worth than all of nature? And what of the love that makes us co-redeemers with Christ, what of those blissful tears through which His peace enters into our soul? The new gnosis is, like all other gnoses, 'a poor gnosis.'[147]

Teilhard inverts the hierarchy of values

Teilhard completely reverses the Christian hierarchy of values. For him, cosmic processes rank higher than the individual soul. Research and work rank higher than moral values. Action as such (that is, any association with the evolutionary process) is more important than contemplation, contrition for our sins, and penance. Progress in the conquest and "totalization" of the world through evolution ranks higher than holiness.

The vast gulf between Teilhard's world and the Christian world is dramatically clear when we compare Cardinal Newman's priorities with Teilhard's. Newman says:

> Saintly purity, saintly poverty, renouncement of the world, the favor of Heaven, the protection of the angels, the smile of the blessed Mary, the gifts of grace, the interposition of miracles, the intercommunion of merits, these are the high and precious things, the things to be looked up to, the things to be reverently spoken of.[148]

[147] *Le paysan de la Garonne*, 181-82.

[148] John Henry Cardinal Newman, *Discourses Addressed to Mixed Congregations* (London: Longmans, 1916), 94.

But for Teilhard it is otherwise:

> To adore once meant to prefer God to things by referring them to Him and by sacrificing them to Him. Adoring today becomes giving oneself body and soul to the creator — associating ourselves with the creator — in order to give the finishing touch to the world through work and research.[149]

Teilhardism is incompatible with Christianity

Teilhard's ambiguous use of classical Christian terms cannot conceal the basic meaning and direction of his thought. It is impossible, therefore, to agree with Henri de Lubac that Teilhard's theology fiction is a "possible" addition to Christian revelation.[150] Evidence compels agreement with Philippe de la Trinité that it is "a deformation of Christianity, which is transformed into an evolutionism of the naturalistic, monistic, and pantheistic brand."[151]

Teilhard's theories are based in equivocations

In his works, he glides from one notion to another, creating a cult of equivocation deeply linked with his monistic ideal. He systematically blurs decisive differences such as that between hope and optimism, and Christian love of neighbor (essentially directed to an individual person) and infatuation with humanity (in which the individual is but a single unit of the species *man*). He ignores

[149]"*Christologie et évolution*" (unpublished), as quoted in Garaudy, "Le Père Teilhard, le concile et les marxistes," *Europe*, No. 431-32 (1965): 192.

[150]Henri de Lubac, *La pensée religieuse du Père Teilhard de Chardin* (Paris: Aubier, 1962).

[151]*Rome et Teilhard de Chardin* (Paris: Arthème Fayard, 1964), 38. Père de la Trinité's study is quite valuable.

the difference between eternity and the earthly future of humanity, and fuses both in the totalization of the Christ-Omega. There is something touching in his desperate effort to combine a traditional, emotional attraction to the Church with a theology radically opposed to its doctrine. But this apparent devotion to Christian terms makes him more dangerous than Voltaire, Renan, or Nietzsche. His success in wrapping a pantheistic, gnostic monism in Christian garments is most evident in *The Divine Milieu*.

Teilhard substitutes efficiency for sanctity

To many readers, the terms Teilhard uses sound so familiar that they exclaim: how can you accuse him of not being an orthodox? Does he not say in *The Divine Milieu*, "What is it for a person to be a saint if not, in effect, to adhere to God with all his power?" This sounds absolutely orthodox. Nonetheless, his notion of adhering to God hides a shift from the heroic virtues of the saint to collaboration in evolution. Attaining holiness in the moral sphere through obeying God's commands and imitating Christ is tacitly replaced by emphasis on developing man's faculties with (and the word seems appropriate) efficiency. This is clearly the case, although Teilhard veils the point in traditional terminology:

> What is it to adhere to God fully if not to fulfill in the world organized around Christ the exact function, humble or important, to which nature and supernature destine it?[152]

For Teilhard, the meaning of the individual lies in his fulfillment of a function in the whole, in the evolutionary process. The individual is no longer called to glorify God through that imitation of Christ which is the one common goal for every true Christian.

[152] *The Divine Milieu* (New York: Harper, 1960), 36.

Teilhard's "religion" is worldly

The transposition of the Cross into the Christ-Omega is also wrapped in apparently traditional terms:

> Toward the summit, wrapped in mist to our human eyes and to which the Cross invites us, we rise by a path which is the way of universal Progress. The royal road of the Cross is no more nor less than the road of human endeavor supernaturally righted and prolonged.[153]

Here, Christian symbols conceal a radical transformation of Christianity that takes us out of the Christian orbit altogether into a completely different spiritual climate. Sometimes, however, Teilhard does discard the Christian guise, and openly reveals his true stand. In 1934, in China, he wrote:

> If in consequence of some inner revolution, I were to lose my faith in Christ, my faith in a personal God, my faith in the spirit, it seems to me that I would continue to have faith in the world. The world (the value, infallibility, and goodness of the world) this is — definitely — the first and only thing in which I believe.[154]

Teilhard's optimism wins converts to his views

Yet, clear as is the heterodoxy of Teilhard's theology, some Catholics have elevated him to the rank of a Doctor and even a Father of the Church. For many unsophisticated Catholics, he has

[153]Ibid., 78.

[154]"Comment je crois" (unpublished), as quoted in Philippe de la Trinité, *Rome et Teilhard de Chardin*, 190.

become a kind of prophet. That progressive Catholics relish Teilhard is, of course, not surprising. The "new theologians" and the "new moralists" welcome Teilhard's views because they share his historical relativism and his conviction that faith must be adapted to modern man. Indeed, for many progressive Catholics, Teilhard's transposition of Christian revelation does not go far enough.

It is astonishing, too, that many faithful Christians are carried away by Teilhard and fail to grasp the complete incompatibility of his teaching with the doctrine of the Church. This popularity, however, is less surprising when seen in the context of our contemporary intellectual and moral climate. In a time familiar with Sartre's "nausea" and Heidegger's conception of the essentially "homeless" man, Teilhard's radiant, optimistic outlook comes for many as a welcome relief. His claim that we are constantly collaborating with God (whatever we do and however insignificant our role) and that "everything is sacred" understandably exhilarates many depressed souls. Another reason for enthusiasm — perhaps more important — is that Teilhard is credited with having overcome a narrow asceticism and false supernaturalism.

Teilhard claims Catholicism disparages nature

Many pious Catholics in earlier generations did view natural goods primarily as potential dangers that threatened to divert them from God. Natural goods — even those endowed with high values (such as beauty in nature and in art, natural truth, and human love) — were approached with suspicion. These Catholics overlooked the positive value that natural goods have for man. They often argued that natural goods should only be *used*, but they should never evoke interest and appreciation for their own sake.

In this, they forgot the fundamental difference between *natural* goods and *worldly* goods (such as wealth, fame, or success). They forgot that natural goods, endowed as they are with intrinsic value, should not only be used by man, but also appreciated for their own sake; and that it is only worldly goods that should be used.

It cannot be denied, moreover, that this unfortunate oversimplification often gained currency in seminaries and monasteries, notwithstanding the fact that it was never part of the doctrine of the Church.

This is why Teilhard can with superficial plausibility accuse the Catholic tradition of disparaging nature; and because he himself praises nature, it is understandable that for many, his thought has seemed to be a just appreciation of natural goods.

Teilhard accuses Christianity of dehumanizing man

Teilhard's related claim that traditional Christianity has created a gap between humanness and Christian perfection has also impressed many sincere Catholics. In *The Divine Milieu* he attributes to traditional Christianity the notion that "men must put off their human garments in order to be Christians."[155]

Again, it cannot be denied that Jansenism reflects this attitude or that certain Jansenistic tendencies have crept anonymously into the minds of many Catholics. For instance, the arch-Christian doctrine that insists that we must die to ourselves in order to be transformed in Christ has often been given an unwarranted dehumanizing emphasis in certain religious institutions. The view has been encouraged in some monasteries and seminaries that nature must, in effect, be killed before the supernatural life of grace can blossom. In the official doctrine of the Church, however, such dehumanization is flatly rejected. As Pope Pius XII said:

[155]*The Divine Milieu*, 34.

> Grace does not destroy nature; it does not even change it; it transfigures it. Indeed, dehumanization is so far from being required for Christian perfection that this may be said: only the person who is transformed in Christ embodies the true fulfillment of his human personality.[156]

Teilhard's own theories dehumanize man

Our point is that Teilhard himself ignores the value of high natural goods and, contrary to his claim, a real dehumanization takes place in his monistic pantheism. We have seen that his ideal of collective man and superhumanity necessarily implies a blindness to the real nature of the individual person and, derivatively, to all the plenitude of human life. But dehumanization also follows inevitably from his monism which minimizes the real drama of human life — the fight between good and evil — and reduces antithetical differences to mere gradations of a continuum.

Teilhard misses the supernatural aspect of natural goods

Teilhard's failure to do justice to the true significance of natural goods is clear the very moment he stresses their importance for eternity. For in dealing with natural goods he is primarily concerned with human activities, with accomplishments in work and research. He does not mention the higher natural goods and the message of God they contain, but only activities, performances, and accomplishments in the natural field. Teilhard applies to these actions the biblical words "His deeds follow them" (*opera ejus sequuntur illos)*, but he does so in contradistinction to the original

[156]*The Pope Speaks: the Teachings of Pope Pius XII*, ed. Michael Chinigo (New York: Pantheon, 1957).

meaning of *opera*, in which "works" are identical with *morally significant deeds*.[157]

Still more important is the relation he sees between natural goods as such and God. Teilhard sees no message of God's glory in the values contained in these great natural goods; nor does he find in them a personal experience of the voice of God. Instead, he posits an objective and unexperienced link between God and our activities that results from the *concursus divinus*. He says: "God is, in a way, at the end of my pen, of my pickax, of my paintbrush, of my sewing needle, of my heart, of my thought."[158]

The real object of Teilhard's boundless enthusiasm, then, is not natural goods themselves, but an abstraction: the hypothesis of evolution. The nature that moves him is not the colorful, resounding beauty of which all the great poets sing. It is not the nature of Dante, Shakespeare, Keats, Goethe, Hölderlin, Leopardi. It is not the glory of a sunrise or a sunset, or the star-studded sky — the evidences of the natural world which Kant regarded, along with the moral law in man's breast, as the most sublime thing of all.

Teilhard levels the hierarchy of values

In another way, Teilhard's ideas necessarily result in dehumanization of the cosmos and man's life. In his world view there is no place for an antithesis of values and disvalues. Yet every attempt to deny these ultimately important qualitative antagonisms always produces a leveling, even a nihilism. This also occurs when the *hierarchy* of values is overlooked, if only because man then responds to all levels of value with the same degree of enthusiasm.

[157]Rev. 14:13. See *The Divine Milieu*, 24.
[158]*The Divine Milieu*, 33.

The principle "everything is sacred," which sounds so uplifting and exhilarating, is in reality fraught with a nihilistic denial of low and high, of good and evil. This fallacious and treacherous approach of praising everything actually results in denying everything. It reminds me of a remark made by a violinist I once met. "I love music so much," he said, "that I do not care what kind of music it is, as long as it is music." This statement, designed to suggest an extraordinary love for music, in fact revealed an absence of any true understanding of music and therefore of any capacity to love music. The same thing happens to man when qualitative distinctions are not made.

Let us now examine the Christian view of nature compared to that of Teilhard. The Christian tradition has always affirmed the revelation of God in nature. The *Sanctus* says, "Heaven and earth are full of Your glory." The Psalms are full of praise of God as the Creator of the marvelous features of nature. St. Augustine's exemplarism repeatedly emphasizes the message of God in the beauty of nature. The same idea is found in St. Francis' love of nature.

Teilhard's nature has no transcendent dimension

But an appreciation of this natural revelation of God implies an "upward direction toward God," to use Teilhard's terminology. Natural revelation speaks to us of God by suggesting the admirable wisdom that pervades creation and by providing a reflection, in the values of natural goods, of God's infinite beauty and glory.

Our response to this revelation is either trembling reverence and wonder for the wisdom manifest in the finality of the cosmos and its mysterious plenitude, a looking up to God the Creator, or at least a deep awareness of the beauty of nature and of all the high natural goods. The latter also lifts up our vision. In either case, we are able to grasp the message from above; for all true values are pregnant with a promise of eternity. By lifting up our hearts we are able to understand that these authentic values speak of God's infinite glory. And, of course, all of this unmistakably implies an "upward direction."

But Teilhard's "nature" is not linked to an "upward direction"; it is not a message from above. Since, for Teilhard, God is *behind* nature, we are supposed to reach Him in the Christ-Omega by moving in a "forward direction."

In Teilhard's forward direction, where everything is involved in an evolutionary movement, natural goods lose their real value. The suggestion they contain of something transcendent is replaced by a merely immanent finality; they become links in the chain of evolution.

When evolution is viewed as the main and decisive reality — when it is, in fact, deified — then every natural good becomes, on the one hand, a mere transitory step in the forward movement of the evolutionary process, and on the other hand, a mute thing, cut off by a leveling monism from its real, qualitative, inherent importance.

It follows that we can do justice to high natural goods only if we discern in them a reflection of an infinitely higher reality, a reality ontologically different from them. This "message character" of natural goods is admirably expressed in Cardinal Newman's remarks about music.

> Can it be that those mysterious stirrings of the heart and keen emotion and strange yearnings after we know not what and awful impressions from we know not whence, should be brought in us by what is unsubstantial, and comes and goes, and begins and ends in itself? It is not so; it cannot be. No; they have escaped from some higher sphere, they are the outpourings of eternal harmony in the medium of created

sound; they are echoes of our home; they are the voice of angels, or the Magnificat of the Saints.[159]

Teilhard overvalues industrialization

Another aspect of this problem deserves notice. The fact that Teilhard sees a higher stage of evolution in today's industrialized world reveals his lack of a real sense of the beauty of nature and of the qualitative message of God it bears. Even the most enthusiastic progressive cannot deny that industrialization consistently ruins the beauty of nature.

Moreover, industrialization (although perhaps the process is inevitable) certainly cannot be considered a univocal progress, either from the point of view of increasing human happiness or of fostering higher culture and a real humanism. As Gabriel Marcel correctly shows in his *Man Against Mass Society*, industrialization implies the danger of a progressive dehumanization. The replacement of the "organic" in human life by the artificial — from artificial insemination to social engineering — is symptomatic of this dehumanization.

Yet Teilhard heedlessly jumps from an enthusiasm for nature to elation over the progress of technology and industrialization. We are thus again confronted with his blindness to antitheses, with his monistic leveling.

It is clear, nevertheless, that Teilhard's first love is technological progress. God's creation has to be completed by man — not in St. Paul's sense, not by cooperating with nature,[160] but by replacing nature with the machine.

[159]John Henry Cardinal Newman, *Fifteen Sermons Preached before the University of Oxford* (London: Longmans, 1909), 346-47.

[160]Rom. 8:19-23.

Teilhard does not give the response due to matter and spirit

The poetic expressions that appear when Teilhard presents his vision of evolution and progress make clear that he never saw the authentic poetry of nature or of the classical "forms" of creation. Instead, he tries to project poetry into technology, again revealing a monistic denial of the basic differences between the poetic and prosaic, the organic and the artificial, the sacred and the profane.

To be sure, it is always impressive when a man seems to have achieved a deep vision of being, and, instead of taking it for granted, gives it a full and ardent response. So with Teilhard. We are far from denying that he discovered in matter many aspects which had generally been overlooked. For example, the mysterious structure and the multiplicity of matter, which natural science is increasingly unfolding, call for genuine wonderment about this reality and respect for this creation of God.

But because Teilhard does not recognize the essential differences between spirit and matter and because his response to the spirit is not in proportion to his praise of matter (recall his "prayer" to matter), the advantage of this unusual insight into matter is, for him, quickly lost.[161]

We must put this question of "matter" in its proper perspective. To overlook the marvels hidden in a creature that ranks lowest in the hierarchy of being is regrettable. But the oversight does not affect our knowledge of higher ranking creatures; it is therefore not a catastrophe.

On the other hand, to grasp the lower while overlooking the higher is to distort our entire world view; and that *is* a catastrophe. Moreover, to esteem a lower good as a higher is to misunderstand

[161] See Philippe de la Trinité, *Rome et Teilhard de Chardin*, 180-85.

the hierarchical structure of being and thus to lose the basis for properly evaluating either higher or lower things.

Teilhard's blindness to the real values in, for example, human love is shown in these unfortunate remarks about *eros* and *agape:*

> Naturally, I agree with you that the solution of the *eros-agape* problem is simply to be found in the evolutionary trend (*dans l'évolutif*) in the genetic, that is to say, in sublimation. [It is to be found in] the spirit emerging from matter through the pancosmic operation.[162]

Teilhard misses the grandeur of conscience and morality

We have already seen that Teilhard's conception of the moral sphere (virtue and sin) is incompatible with Christian revelation. We may now note that the role he grants to the moral sphere is yet another factor leading to dehumanization.

The unique contact with God that takes place in one's conscience and in one's awareness of his moral obligations, plays no role in Teilhard's system. He does not understand that man in the realm of nature never reaches so intimate a contact with God as he does when he listens to the voice of his conscience and consciously submits to moral obligation. In comparison, how pale — in purely human and natural terms — is Teilhard's notion of the "conscious" and the "unconscious" participating in a "cosmic progress"!

And how pale are the scope and breadth of cosmic events in contrast with the liberating transcendence of a man authentically contrite! What event could hold more grandeur than David's

[162]Letter of March 13, 1954, in *Psyché*, No. 99-100 (1955): 9. As quoted in *Rome et Teilhard de Chardin*, 58.

response to the challenge of the prophet Nathan? The secondary role which Teilhard assigns to man's conscious and personal dialogue with Christ — Teilhard's preference for objective cooperation in the "evolutionary process" — reveals as clearly as anything can the truly dehumanized character of his "new world."

Many people are impressed by a thinker who constructs a new world out of his own mind in which every thing is interconnected and "explained." They consider such conceptions the most eminent feat of the human mind. Accordingly, they praise Teilhard as a great synthetic thinker. In truth, however, the measure of a thinker's greatness is the extent to which he has grasped reality in its plenitude and depth and in its hierarchical structure. If *this* measure is applied to Teilhard, he obviously cannot be considered a great thinker.

Let us once again dramatize the non-Christian nature of the Teilhardian speculation by comparing his presentation of the meaning and purpose of Christianity with that of Cardinal Newman. Teilhard proclaims that Christ becomes

> the flame of human efforts; He reveals Himself as the form of faith which is most appropriate for modern needs — a religion for progress, the religion even for progress on earth; I dare say: the religion of evolution.[163]

Cardinal Newman, however, reveals the true purpose of our faith:

> St. Paul . . . labored more than all the Apostles; and why? Not to civilize the world, not to smooth the face of society, not to spread abroad knowledge, not to cultivate the reason,

[163]"Quelques réflexions sur la conversion du monde," in *Oeuvres*, vol. 9, *Science et Christ* (Paris: Editions du Seuil, 1964), 166. Also quoted in Garaudy, *Europe*, No. 431-32 (1965): 190.

not for any great worldly object. . . . Not to turn the whole earth into a heaven, but to bring down a heaven upon earth. This has been the real triumph of the Gospel. . . . It has made men saints.[164]

[164]John Henry Cardinal Newman, *Parochial and Plain Sermons*, vol. 4 (London: Longmans, 1900), 151-156.

SOPHIA INSTITUTE PRESS

Sophia Institute is a non-profit institution that seeks to restore man's knowledge of eternal truth, including man's knowledge of his own nature, his relation to other persons, and his relation to God.

Sophia Institute Press serves this end in a number of ways. It publishes translations of foreign works to make them accessible for the first time to English-speaking readers. It brings back into print many books that have long been out of print. And it publishes important new books that fulfill the ideals of Sophia Institute. These books afford readers a rich source of the enduring wisdom of mankind.

Sophia Institute Press makes high-quality books available to the general public by using advanced, cost-effective technology and by soliciting donations to subsidize general publishing costs. Your generosity can help us provide the public with editions of works containing the enduring wisdom of the ages. Please send your tax-deductible contribution to the address noted below. Your questions, comments, and suggestions are also welcome.